New D

Edited by **Gordon Giles**   May–August 2025

7	**1—3 John** Michael Mitton	*1–10 May*
19	**Numbers: further wilderness adventures** Naomi Starkey	*11–24 May*
34	**Luke 13—16** Margaret Silf	*25 May–7 June*
49	**Numbered for God** Gordon Giles	*8–21 June*
64	**Esther** Fiona Stratta	*22 June–5 July*
79	**Peacemaking** Matt McChlery	*6–12 July*
87	**Psalms 67—72** Roland Riem	*13–26 July*
102	**1 Corinthians 1—8** Liz Hoare	*27 July–9 August*
117	**Bible chemicals** Geoffrey Lowson	*10–23 August*
132	**Barnabas** Martin Leckebusch	*24–31 August*

 Ministries

15 The Chambers, Vineyard,
Abingdon OX14 3FE
+44 (0)1865 319700 | brf.org.uk

Bible Reading Fellowship is a charity (233280) and company limited by guarantee (301324), registered in England and Wales

EU Authorised Representative: Easy Access System Europe –
Mustamäe tee 50, 10621 Tallinn, Estonia, **gpsr.requests@easproject.com**

ISBN 978 1 80039 354 7
All rights reserved

This edition © Bible Reading Fellowship 2025
Cover photo by Pixabay/pexels.com

Distributed in Australia by:
MediaCom Education Inc, PO Box 610, Unley, SA 5061
Tel: 1 800 811 311 | admin@mediacom.org.au

Distributed in New Zealand by:
Scripture Union Wholesale, PO Box 760, Wellington 6140
Tel: 04 385 0421 | suwholesale@clear.net.nz

Acknowledgements
Scripture quotations marked with the following abbreviations are taken from the version shown. Where no abbreviation is given, the quotation is taken from the same version as the headline reference. NRSV: the New Revised Standard Version Updated Edition. Copyright © 2021 National Council of Churches of Christ in the United States of America. Used by permission. All rights reserved worldwide. NIV: The Holy Bible, New International Version, Anglicised edition, copyright © 1979, 1984, 2011 by Biblica. Used by permission of Hodder & Stoughton Publishers, an Hachette UK company. All rights reserved. 'NIV' is a registered trademark of Biblica. UK trademark number 1448790. NLT: The Holy Bible, New Living Translation, copyright © 1996, 2004, 2007, 2013. Used by permission of Tyndale House Publishers, Inc., Carol Stream, Illinois 60188. All rights reserved. KJV: The Authorised Version of the Bible (The King James Bible), the rights in which are vested in the Crown, are reproduced by permission of the Crown's Patentee, Cambridge University Press. REB: the Revised English Bible, copyright © Cambridge University Press and Oxford University Press 1989. All rights reserved. TNIV: The Holy Bible, Today's New International Version, copyright © 2004 by Biblica. Used by permission of Hodder & Stoughton Publishers, a division of Hodder Headline Ltd. All rights reserved. 'TNIV' is a registered trademark of International Bible Society.

A catalogue record for this book is available from the British Library

Printed and bound in the UK by Zenith Media NP4 0DQ

Suggestions for using *New Daylight*

Find a regular time and place, if possible, where you can read and pray undisturbed. Before you begin, take time to be still and perhaps use the prayer of BRF Ministries on page 6. Then read the Bible passage slowly (try reading it aloud if you find it over-familiar), followed by the comment. You can also use *New Daylight* for group study and discussion, if you prefer.

The prayer or point for reflection can be a starting point for your own meditation and prayer. Many people like to keep a journal to record their thoughts about a Bible passage and items for prayer. In *New Daylight* we also note the Sundays and some special festivals from the church calendar, to keep in step with the Christian year.

New Daylight and the Bible

New Daylight contributors use a range of Bible versions, and you will find a list of the versions used opposite. You are welcome to use your own preferred version alongside the passage printed in the notes. This can be particularly helpful if the Bible text has been abridged.

New Daylight affirms that the whole of the Bible is God's revelation to us, and we should read, reflect on and learn from every part of both Old and New Testaments. Usually the printed comment presents a straightforward 'thought for the day', but sometimes it may also raise questions rather than simply providing answers, as we wrestle with some of the more difficult passages of scripture.

New Daylight is also available in a deluxe edition (larger format). Visit your local Christian bookshop or BRF's online shop **brfonline.org.uk**. To obtain an audio version for the blind or partially sighted, contact Torch Trust for the Blind, Torch House, Torch Way, Northampton Road, Market Harborough LE16 9HL; +44 (0)1858 438260; **info@torchtrust.org**.

Comment on *New Daylight*

To send feedback, please email **enquiries@brf.org.uk**, phone **+44 (0)1865 319700** or write to the address shown opposite.

Writers in this issue

Liz Hoare works part-time at the St Bede's Pastoral Centre in York, which offers spiritual accompaniment, training and quiet days. Liz has written two books – *Using the Bible in Spiritual Direction* and *Twelve Great Women Writers* – and is currently working on a book about contentment.

Martin Leckebusch worked in IT for 37 years before retiring to spend more time writing. He lives in Gloucester, is an elder at a Baptist church and is the author of over 500 published hymn texts.

Geoffrey Lowson is a retired priest living in a small village in the west of County Durham. In addition to parochial ministry, he spent 21 years working for the mission agency USPG.

Matt McChlery is an author, songwriter and overseer (elder) of his local church. He has written four books, the most recent being *The Prison Letters: A 40 day devotional for Lent*. He is also host of the 'Christian Book Blurb' podcast, which aims to help listeners in their discipleship one book at a time.

Michael Mitton is a freelance writer, speaker and spiritual director. He is also a canon emeritus of Derby Cathedral. His books include *The Poetry of Pilgrimage* and *Restoring the Woven Cord*, both published by BRF Ministries.

Roland Riem is vice dean of Winchester Cathedral. He is involved in the greening of the cathedral and the development of its interpretation for visitors. In previous roles Roland was involved in university chaplaincy and theological education.

Margaret Silf is an ecumenical Christian committed to working across and beyond traditional divisions. She is the author of a number of books for 21st-century spiritual pilgrims and a retreat facilitator.

Naomi Starkey is vicar (ministry area leader) of Bro Eryri, six worshipping communities in the shadow of Yr Wyddfa (Snowdon) in north Wales.

Fiona Stratta worked as a speech and language therapist and now works as a tutor and speech and drama teacher. She is author of *Walking with Gospel Women* and *Walking with Biblical Women of Courage*, both published by BRF.

Gordon Giles writes...

In this summer's edition of *New Daylight* we have a few sets of thematic reflections alongside our usual extracts from biblical books. Psalms, gospel and Old Testament passages are interspersed with the themes of chemistry, numbers and peacemaking as well as an encounter with Barnabas. Consequently there is one short passage that occurs twice in this edition. Appearing as part of two sets of readings drawn from across the Bible, our authors' reflections on it are very different. I wonder if you can spot it!

It goes to show how deep, how wide, how broad and how universal is the word of God. So much can be extrapolated from a brief passage of scripture. This is the nature and purpose of *New Daylight*, that just a few lines can feed us for the day. Our authors have been serving us biblical morsels for many years now, and the recipe still satisfies our hunger for the word and grace of God. While the Bible is inexhaustible, it does, after all, only have 66 books, and so we often find ourselves encountering familiar books or texts if we read for many years, as many readers do and have done. Yet the gift of God's word to us is the gift that keeps giving, often in new and creative ways. Sometimes putting passages from different parts of the Bible together thematically can yield fresh insights, while a continuous read-through is a good discipline too.

While God's word is unchanging, and Jesus Christ is the same yesterday, today and tomorrow, we are not. Life happens, and it changes us. The living, the loving, the losing and the leaving behind affect us and change us, as do world events. When we read a passage of scripture, it is the same as when we last read it, but we and the world are not. Therefore, we might read it differently and God speaks to us through it in new ways. This can be enlightening or painful. When we engage our minds and spirits with scripture in new ways we expose our inner selves to the Spirit of God, speaking through the Bible, and this is a form of vulnerable submission to Christ. Yet in doing so, by his grace we open ourselves to challenge, comfort, enlightenment and blessing.

GORDON GILES

The prayer of BRF Ministries

Faithful God,
thank you for growing BRF
from small beginnings
into the worldwide family of BRF Ministries.
We rejoice as young and old
discover you through your word
and grow daily in faith and love.
Keep us humble in your service,
ambitious for your glory
and open to new opportunities.
For your name's sake,
Amen.

'It is such a joy to be part of this amazing project'

As part of our Living Faith ministry, we're raising funds to give away copies of Bible reading notes and other resources to those who aren't able to access them any other way, working with food banks and chaplaincy services, in prisons, hospitals and care homes.

'This very generous gift will be hugely appreciated, and truly bless each recipient… Bless you for your kindness.'

'We would like to send our enormous thanks to all involved. Your generosity will have a significant impact and will help us to continue to provide support to local people in crisis, and for this we cannot thank you enough.'

If you've enjoyed and benefited from our resources, would you consider paying it forward to enable others to do so too?

Make a gift at **brf.org.uk/donate**

Introduction

1—3 John

Towards the end of the New Testament we find three letters traditionally attributed to John, the author of the fourth gospel. The author is not named, but there are certainly resonances with the gospel, and for our daily readings I shall run with the tradition that John is our author. He is an old man, writing at the end of the first century. He opens his first letter telling his readers that he was actually there with Jesus, and there can't have been many left at this time who could testify to that. John could describe the look in his eye, the sound of his voice and the feel of his hand. In his letters, we sense an urgency in reminding his readers that this Jesus was real, for heresies are developing which are starting to present very skewed views of God and Christ. John wants to bring his readers back to basics, and he does this with clarity and winsomeness.

When I read through these letters in one sitting, I found that certain words caught my attention. They were such familiar words that I was in danger of ignoring them. Familiarity with such words breeds not so much contempt as boredom. Words can get very tired when they are used often, and religious words particularly so, not least because so often they have been weighed down with hefty, polemical punches delivered from pulpits. Words like 'sin' feel grim. 'Light' too often becomes a cliché. And the poor word 'love' looks completely exhausted. But reading through the letters of John, I found these tired, old words sprung back to life, as if someone had given them a good watering.

In the coming days I have picked out ten of these words, exploring how John has used them to encourage not only his early readers but also us, who 2,000 years on still struggle with much the same issues as those early Christians did – managing our wounded and frail humanity and trying to make sense of these precious lives we have been given. John brings us back to basics, the main basic being the life of Jesus, who is *the* Word.

MICHAEL MITTON

Thursday 1 May   **1 John 1:1–3 (NRSV)**

Life

We declare to you what was from the beginning, what we have heard, what we have seen with our eyes, what we have looked at and touched with our hands, concerning the word of life – this life was revealed, and we have seen it and testify to it and declare to you the eternal life that was with the Father and was revealed to us – what we have seen and heard we also declare to you so that you also may have fellowship with us, and truly our fellowship is with the Father and with his Son Jesus Christ.

What a magnificent start to a letter! You can feel the strength of the spirit of John as he declares so confidently: 'I have seen it; I have heard it; I have touched it.' There can be no disputing his evidence.

Evidence for what? For life. Here we have our first word. John gets straight to the point at the outset of his letter – we are talking about life here and a life that stretches right back to the beginning. As with the gospel, the opening sentence takes us to the creation of all things – the moment when God spoke his word and energised life on this planet. We remember the story of how God created humans from the dust of the ground and marvellously animated that dust by his breath. This is primal life. The memory of creation alerts us to the true wonder of this life.

But then, says John, he witnessed this life even more vividly. He actually saw, heard and felt it in one of his fellow humans: Jesus of Nazareth. And John is telling his readers that it is through Jesus' ministry, death and resurrection that a whole new quality of life was revealed – eternal life. Several times in his letter, he returns to the glorious truth that this eternal life has been promised to us (1 John 2:25; 5:13).

Lovers of *Star Trek* will remember the phrase attributed to Spock in the 1987 song 'Star Trekkin'', sung by The Firm: 'It's life, Jim, but not as we know it.' John is inviting us all to let go of our old, tired concepts of life, and discover the vibrant, God-breathed, eternal life revealed in Jesus. It's life, Jim – but much more than we know it.

Father in heaven, open my eyes and heart to experience this gift of eternal life. Amen.

MICHAEL MITTON

Friday 2 May   **1 John 1:5–7 (NRSV)**

Light

This is the message we have heard from him and proclaim to you, that God is light and in him there is no darkness at all. If we say that we have fellowship with him while we are walking in darkness, we lie and do not do what is true; but if we walk in the light as he himself is in the light, we have fellowship with one another, and the blood of Jesus his Son cleanses us from all sin.

We are still in the opening sentences of John's first letter, and he is writing about one of his favourite themes, namely the theme of light (a prominent theme also in John's gospel). As with the theme of life, we have another primal theme here. In the opening verses of Genesis, we have a world that is in the dark until it is transformed by God's command, 'Let there be light' (Genesis 1:3). This powerful imagery of light and dark runs throughout the Bible. It is one so easy for sighted people to recognise. Life is difficult if we cannot see what we are doing or where we are going.

It is believed that one of John's concerns when writing his letters was regarding the growth of a heresy that is known generally as Gnosticism. One feature of this was the belief that some privileged people were allowed access to enlightened knowledge – they were perceived as the clever, inspired ones who had the light to shine on your darkness. Some were taken in by this. However, says John, there is one sure test that provides evidence of true light: it is the quality of relationships. One of the sure evidences that someone is 'in the light' is how they treat their fellow humans. One of the effects of this light is the forming of a healthy community.

John uses the expression 'walk in the light', which is really a spiritual discipline. It requires us to develop an instinct that detects the light of Christ and makes choices to walk where we find such light. A key indicator of knowing that we are walking in the light is the way we relate to others.

Lord Jesus, you are the light of the world.
Enlighten my heart and mind today. Amen.

MICHAEL MITTON

Saturday 3 May   **1 John 2:12–14 (NRSV)**

Evil

I am writing to you, little children, because your sins are forgiven on account of his name. I am writing to you, fathers, because you know him who is from the beginning. I am writing to you, young people, because you have conquered the evil one. I write to you, children, because you know the Father. I write to you, fathers, because you know him who is from the beginning. I write to you, young people, because you are strong and the word of God abides in you, and you have overcome the evil one.

Having given thought to the light, we now turn our attention to the dark. There is much in John's letters about evil. He sees the world as a tripartite drama involving God, humans and the evil one (which he sometimes calls 'the devil'). He has a clear understanding that 'the whole world lies under the power of the evil one' (1 John 5:19). But in today's passage he declares very clearly that it is quite possible to overcome the power of the evil one. The reason for this confidence is declared in 1 John 3:8: 'The Son of God was revealed for this purpose: to destroy the works of the devil.' John is making clear that a primary purpose of the coming of Christ was to destroy the power of evil that has gripped this world.

   Humanity has always been fascinated with the concept of evil, and we do not have to look far in our world to see what grim havoc evil has caused. John is not shy of discussing this fearful power of evil, but he is quick to point out that the followers of Christ are those who take on evil. He sees it as a natural part of their discipleship. This is still our responsibility. The overcoming of evil does not require great contests of high drama – it is often overcome by the little things. Every prayer of faith, every act of goodness, every word of forgiveness, every challenging of injustice, every work of compassion – all such things are powerful lights that overcome the dark evil active in this world.

Lord of heaven, embolden and equip me to challenge the works of darkness that cause such turmoil in our world. Amen.

MICHAEL MITTON

Sunday 4 May — **1 John 2:15–17 (CEB)**

World

Don't love the world or the things in the world. If anyone loves the world, the love of the Father is not in them. Everything that is in the world – the craving for whatever the body feels, the craving for whatever the eyes see and the arrogant pride in one's possessions – is not of the Father but is of the world. And the world and its cravings are passing away, but the person who does the will of God remains forever.

Probably the most famous verse in the Bible is John 3:16, which begins 'God so loved the world…' It is a little confusing therefore to read in today's passage that we are told *not* to love the world. The same Greek word, *kosmos*, is used in both gospel and epistle.

So how are we to understand this? In the gospel, it is emphatically clear that God's disposition towards this world and the human race is one of love. He loves this world so much that one day he will return and make his home here (Revelation 21:3). However, in John's letters the world is viewed as hostile, because he sees it as being occupied by an alien power. The world has been drastically infected by 'the antichrist' (1 John 4:3), so much so that within this world lie insidious powers that threaten humanity. Thus healthy appetites become damaging cravings, and possessions are not gifts to steward, but things used to boost our pride.

Over the centuries Christians have sometimes demonstrated such an adversarial approach to the world that they have denied the many good things in this world that are still uncorrupted. Furthermore, they can detach themselves from the world rather than seeking to transform it by God's love and power. John's antipathy is towards the power of evil that has so corrupted this world, and he warns us to be on our guard. But none of this takes away from the fact that God deeply loves this world, and our calling is to engage with him in working for its healing and freeing those who have been captured by the darkness operating in the world.

Lord Jesus, free me from the powers that corrupt
and use me as an agent of your healing. Amen.

MICHAEL MITTON

Monday 5 May   **1 John 2:24–27 (NRSV)**

Abide

Let what you heard from the beginning abide in you. If what you heard from the beginning abides in you, then you will abide in the Son and in the Father. And this is what he has promised us, eternal life. I write these things to you concerning those who would deceive you. As for you, the anointing that you received from him abides in you, and so you do not need anyone to teach you. But as his anointing teaches you about all things and is true and is not a lie, and just as it has taught you, abide in him.

In these few verses, the word 'abide' appears five times: the good news abides in the believer (twice); the believer abides in Christ (twice); and the anointing abides in the believer. The Greek is *meno*, close to our word 'remain' (a word used in some translations), and John uses it several times more in his letters. In other words, he is fond of this word!

    Abiding is a word we associate with home. Thus John wants his readers to make the gospel fully at home in their hearts. Once they have welcomed the gospel in this way, its power will get to work in them and will give them an awareness that they in turn are at home with the Son and the Father. Then there is this reference to the anointing. In the Old Testament, the practice of anointing with oil signified the empowering and authoritative presence of the Holy Spirit. The context for this passage is a warning about false teachers. Intentional abiding in Christ is a sure safeguard against being drawn into false doctrines and practices. John is commending a lifestyle whereby, confident in making our home with Christ, we in turn fully welcome the gospel and the Spirit.

    John's fondness for this word 'abide' suggests that the workings of the Christian faith are based in an experience of being fully at home. We don't just have a head knowledge of Christ; we live in his home as part of his family. In turn, the gospel and Spirit are not interesting concepts, they are to be welcomed to the hearth of our hearts.

Holy Spirit, usher me today to be at home with Christ. Amen.

MICHAEL MITTON

Tuesday 6 May 1 John 3:1–3 (NRSV)

Children

See what love the Father has given us, that we should be called children of God, and that is what we are. The reason the world does not know us is that it did not know him. Beloved, we are God's children now; what we will be has not yet been revealed. What we do know is this: when he is revealed, we will be like him, for we will see him as he is. And all who have this hope in him purify themselves, just as he is pure.

Frequently in John's letters he addresses his readers as 'children'. In today's passage he wants his readers to fully appreciate what it means to be a child of God. John is commending a God who is not an impersonal deity who commands respect and demands sacrifices to keep us on his good side. Rather, God is a heavenly Father who is proud to call us his children. To know we are beloved of God is the source of our deepest security.

But John says that it does not stop there. Children grow up. What we are now is only a beginning. Those who have young children know well that experience of looking at a young child and speculating what they will be like when they grow up. John says that what we will be has not yet been revealed, but we can hold on to a wonderful hope, which is the knowledge that God's intention is that as we grow up we become more and more like Christ.

We are always children in the sense that we belong to God and are part of his family. But we are not to remain childish all our days. The Christian life is about getting so acquainted with Jesus that we develop his qualities of love, grace, wisdom, justice and so on. Thus John can say, 'Little children, let us love… in deed and truth' (1 John 3:18). The children of God grow by knowing they are beloved and by loving.

Maybe there was another thing in John's mind. Children love to play, and perhaps John desired that the followers of Christ would always be marvellously playful!

Father, free me to live and behave today as your child. Amen.

MICHAEL MITTON

Wednesday 7 May   **1 John 3:4–8a (NRSV)**

Sin

Everyone who commits sin is guilty of lawlessness; sin is lawlessness. You know that he was revealed to take away sins, and in him there is no sin. No one who abides in him sins; no one who sins has either seen him or known him. Little children, let no one deceive you. Everyone who does what is right is righteous, just as he is righteous. Everyone who commits sin is a child of the devil; for the devil has been sinning from the beginning.

The word 'sin' is one of those which never seems to do the job it is supposed to. Outside the church the word is usually used in a jokey way; inside the church it is usually used either formally and rather limply in the context of a confession near the start of a service or it used by a preacher, generally causing the congregation to squirm a little. John, however, is very confident using the word, and it crops up often in his first letter.

At face value, passages like today's are pretty scary. If everyone who sins is a child of the devil, what hope is there for any of us? A closer look at the Greek of the text shows us that the sense of the verb here is an ongoing one. This is about the person who has chosen to deliberately live in opposition to the ways of God and persists in wilfully sinning. Such people, says John, choose not to live as a child of God the Father, but are under the influence of a darker household.

John's reason in writing so starkly is to awaken us to the reality of the situation. To which family do we wish to belong, the family of light or of darkness? Do we want the family traits of Christ or of the evil one? John is speaking to a people who are compromising their values, and he is urging them to resist the power of sin and surrender to the life-giving power of Christ.

The purpose of the word 'sin' is to bring us to our senses. It is not there to condemn us, but to rouse us to live as the children of light.

Lord, today I choose to live as a child of God. Amen.

MICHAEL MITTON

Thursday 8 May   **1 John 4:1–4 (NRSV, abridged)**

Spirit

Beloved, do not believe every spirit, but test the spirits to see whether they are from God, for many false prophets have gone out into the world. By this you know the Spirit of God: every spirit that confesses that Jesus Christ has come in the flesh is from God, and every spirit that does not confess Jesus is not from God. And this is the spirit of the antichrist, of which you have heard that it is coming, and now it is already in the world… The one who is in you is greater than the one who is in the world.

'Spirit' is another word that crops up often in John's first letter, and today's passage gives us his thoughts on the spirit world in concentrated form. Here we have reference to several types of spirits, some of whom are from God and some not. He includes mention of both the spirit of the antichrist and the great Spirit of God.

To the modern materialist, all this will appear complete nonsense! But in the first century, people were comfortable with a view of a world full of all kinds of spirits that made their presence felt in different ways. Generally people were scared of these unseen forces and felt they had little power over them. John encourages the Christians not to be afraid of such spirits, but to be *discerning* – to ascertain what is from God and what is not.

Having taken us into the arena of the spirit world, John then says that the key criterion for testing the spirits is paradoxically to do with the down-to-earth flesh and blood of Christ. He is countering those who are deviating from the fundamental conviction that God became human – the Word has become flesh. John is helping those early Christians into an integrated understanding of the seen and the unseen realities of this world. He invites us into a world view that acknowledges the presence of these unseen forces, but not in a way that disengages us from the material world. And, he says, there is no cause for fear. For the One who is in us is by far the stronger power.

---

*Open my eyes, Lord, that I may spy the things
of both earth and heaven. Amen.*

MICHAEL MITTON

Friday 9 May   **2 John 1:4–6 (NRSV)**

Love

I was overjoyed to find some of your children walking in the truth, just as we have been commanded by the Father. But now, dear lady, I ask you, not as though I were writing you a new commandment but one we have had from the beginning: let us love one another. And this is love, that we walk according to his commandments; this is the commandment just as you have heard it from the beginning – you must walk in it.

John's letters are drenched in references to love. He does not use *philia*, the more common Greek word for love, but *agapē*, which was less common in the Greek-speaking world but is used frequently in the New Testament. *Philia* is the word that conveys warmth and affection. *Agapē* love is not to do with the feelings, but much more to do with the mind and the will. So, in our passage today John is not urging his readers to muster up strong feelings of affection for their fellow believers. Rather he uses this analogy of walking: just as we make a choice to walk in the light, we also make a deliberate decision to walk in the pathway of love.

Once again, it is heartening to think that this early Christian community was facing similar challenges to us today. This challenge is of having to get on with people we find objectionable! But as John points out, we have no choice in this matter. It is a commandment not an aspiration, and in obeying this commandment, the Christian community demonstrates the character of God, and that character is love (1 John 4:8). A church without love is missing the whole point.

It is curious how we can be strangely tolerant of the absence of this love in our churches. Perhaps it is viewed as being too difficult a mountain to climb. Or maybe we feel we lose more than we gain by extending love to those who threaten us. But, says John, such love comes naturally when we know we are beloved of God (1 John 4:19). This is one good reason for spending time in the presence of God.

'Come down, O love divine, seek thou this soul of mine'
(Bianco da Siena, c. 1350–1434). Amen.

MICHAEL MITTON

Saturday 10 May   **3 John 1:2–5, 8 (NRSV)**

Truth

Beloved, I pray that all may go well with you and that you may be in good health, just as it is well with your soul. For I was overjoyed when some brothers and sisters arrived and testified to your faithfulness to the truth, how you walk in the truth. I have no greater joy than this, to hear that my children are walking in the truth. Beloved, you do faithfully whatever you do for the brothers and sisters, even though they are strangers to you… Therefore we ought to support such people, so that we may become coworkers with the truth.

The third letter of John is written to Gaius, who is the devoted pastor of a church. John has heard good reports of how he welcomed some travelling missionaries. What particularly thrills John is to hear of how dedicated Gaius is to 'the truth', a word mentioned no less than four times in this opening of his letter. This takes on more meaning later, when John tackles the issue of a character in the church called Diotrephes, who will not acknowledge John's authority (v. 9) and is spreading false rumours about him. By contrast, John commends a man called Demetrius, who has the marks of truth about him (v. 12). The particular untruth that Diotrephes is dealing in is false accusations about John (v. 10). His motivations for casting these rumours seem to be all to do with his wanting power and influence in the church.

It is interesting to note that John does not become self-defensive, but simply urges Gaius to 'walk in the truth'. Again we are back with John's favourite image of walking. This is the deliberate stepping on to the right pathways. In some ways it is comforting to know that even in the heady days of the first century, they also struggled with powerful personalities trying to control the church. John's advice about this is clear: do not be driven by either your desire for power nor your need to defend yourself. Rather, give all you have to seek the pathway of truth, and then humbly and joyfully walk it.

Lord Jesus, mould my heart that I may discern the ways of truth. Amen.

MICHAEL MITTON

If you've enjoyed this set of reflections by **Michael Mitton**,
check out his books published with BRF Ministries, including...

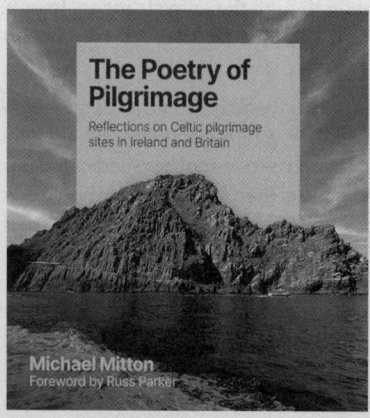 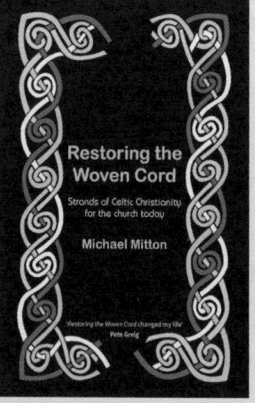

The Poetry of Pilgrimage
Reflections on Celtic pilgrimage sites in Ireland and Britain

978 1 80039 321 9
£12.99

Restoring the Woven Cord
Strands of Celtic Christianity for the church today

978 0 85746 862 8
£9.99

To order, visit **brfonline.org.uk** or use the order form at the end.

Introduction

Numbers: further wilderness adventures

If there were a league of 'least known books of the Bible', it is safe to say that the book of Numbers would be somewhere near the top. There is the title, for a start. When I worked in publishing, colleagues and I would often spend considerable time discussing the best title for a forthcoming book. A good title had to give an idea of the contents, of course, but also appeal to prospective readers. While there are certainly a lot of numbers in Numbers, there is also plenty of drama and controversy. There are stories involving a bronze serpent, a talking donkey and a giant bunch of grapes. Arguably a better title for the book might be 'Further wilderness adventures of the children of Israel'.

As well as being among the least known, Numbers is also one of the more difficult parts of the Bible. It seldom appears among the readings chosen for public worship. Even if we skim through the census lists and the lengthy liturgical guidance, we may well struggle with the stories of violent conquest and what is known today as 'ethnic cleansing'. As modern-day disciples we will find ourselves wrestling with sections of our scriptures. We will find ourselves questioning the assumptions and challenging the values of the narrative, asking of it (and ourselves): 'What is the Spirit saying to the church here?' Presented with yet another tale of panic, plague and destruction, we cannot declare: 'This is the word of the Lord' as if receiving an instruction to 'go and do likewise' (Luke 10:37, NRSV). We need to think, hard.

Our two weeks of readings from the book of Numbers can only offer selected highlights, focusing on some of the better-known episodes at the expense of the chapters of rather repetitive detail. It is worth remembering that, as part of the Pentateuch (the first five books of the Bible), Numbers is a foundational document in many ways and worthy of study for that reason alone. That document may be dark and difficult at times, but it still gives us glimpses of God's purposes and commitment to his chosen people. Those people may be wayward, obstinate and endlessly complaining, but the covenant – even if stretched to breaking point – endures.

NAOMI STARKEY

Sunday 11 May   **Numbers 1:1–3, 18–19 (NRSV, abridged)**

Getting the numbers right

The Lord spoke to Moses in the wilderness of Sinai… in the second year after they had come out of the land of Egypt, saying, 'Take a census of the whole congregation of Israelites, in their clans, by ancestral houses, according to the number of names, every male individually, from twenty years old and up, everyone in Israel able to go to war. You and Aaron shall enrol them, company by company… On the first day of the second month [Moses and Aaron] assembled the whole congregation together. They registered themselves in their clans, by their ancestral houses, according to the number of names from twenty years old and up, individually, as the Lord commanded Moses.

It is more than a year since the Israelites left slavery in Egypt for their journey to freedom and the promised land. Now God commands Moses and his brother Aaron to prepare a census. This is no 'population overview', like the UK's once-a-decade national census. This is a specific reckoning up of the people's potential fighting force. The promised land already has a population – entry will involve physical combat.

The numbers presented are astonishing: more than 600,000 men, a figure which has been used to calculate that the total company must have numbered more than two million. Rather than taking these numbers at face value (and seeking increasingly implausible explanations), an alternative reading is helpfully summarised in Mike Butterworth's *People's Bible Commentary: Leviticus and Numbers* (BRF, 2003). A later scribe misread the Hebrew word for 'chief' as the linguistically similar word for 'thousand', resulting in the inflated total. Reworking the numbers, taking into account the error, produces a more likely total of around 5,550 'battle ready' men.

Today ministers have to keep records of worshipper numbers, not as a possible 'Lord's army' but as a measure of church health. While numbers are not everything, they remind us that each individual matters before God and each plays a unique part in the body of Christ.

'Are not five sparrows sold for two pennies? Yet not one of them is forgotten in God's sight. But even the hairs of your head are all numbered. Do not be afraid; you are of more value than many sparrows' (Luke 12:6–7).

NAOMI STARKEY

Monday 12 May   **Numbers 3:5–9 (NRSV)**

Set apart for service

Then the Lord spoke to Moses, saying, 'Bring the tribe of Levi near and set them before Aaron the priest, so that they may assist him. They shall perform duties for him and for the whole congregation in front of the tent of meeting, doing service at the tabernacle; they shall be in charge of all the furnishings of the tent of meeting and attend to the duties for the Israelites as they do service at the tabernacle. You shall give the Levites to Aaron and his descendants; they are unreservedly given to him from among the Israelites.

Set apart by God for service to the high priest Aaron and his descendants, the tribe of Levi are subject to a separate census which also itemises their tasks (vv. 14–39). A later chapter provides details of their consecration for their sacred duties. At one level they could be seen as privileged; at another level they bear a weighty responsibility in helping to maintain the religious purity of the people. What that responsibility meant is set out at greater length in Leviticus and Deuteronomy, as well as parts of Numbers.

While we do not have to manage a complex sacrificial system, the lives of our worshipping communities still require planning and administration. Besides the rules around finance, safeguarding and so on, there are a host of practical matters, from tidying hymn books to buying toilet paper. After all, even in the time of Aaron in the Sinai wilderness, somebody needed to be 'in charge of all the furnishings'!

I only started to appreciate fully the importance of churchwardens when I became vicar of a group of rural congregations. It is not that the 'person up-front' is too important to deal with such matters – but there are only so many hours in a day (and night). The tireless work of wardens, treasurers, cleaners, welcomers (who may be the same people) is invaluable to the ongoing life of all churches and, just as importantly, the mental and physical health of the minister.

Give thanks for all who volunteer in the life of their local church.
Pray that they may feel valued and that they value their leaders in turn.

NAOMI STARKEY

Tuesday 13 May   **Numbers 6:22–27 (NRSV)**

Threefold blessing

The Lord spoke to Moses, saying, 'Speak to Aaron and his sons, saying: Thus you shall bless the Israelites: You shall say to them: The Lord bless you and keep you; the Lord make his face to shine upon you and be gracious to you; the Lord lift up his countenance upon you and give you peace. So they shall put my name on the Israelites, and I will bless them.'

Known as the Aaronic or priestly blessing, this beautiful prayer is still used regularly in worship by Jewish and Christian believers alike. Its three phrases unfold a pattern that, like a kaleidoscope, turns and turns again to show yet another facet of what blessing means.

In the first phrase, we hear of God's 'keeping' of his people, a word with overtones of safety, protection and shelter. The second phrase (God's face 'shining' upon them) uses the tender image of a face radiant with joy, directed at us as a parent smiles at a darling child. This radiance is paired with grace, the generosity that wants only the best for the beloved.

The final phrase, perhaps most powerful of all, becomes clearer in a different translation: 'The Lord turn his face towards you' (NIV). In the book of Exodus, God tells Moses that 'you cannot see my face, for no one shall see me and live' (33:20). In the words of the priestly blessing, we find the promise that the joyful, loving face of God will shine directly upon his people like the noonday sun.

In the blessing, as throughout the book of Numbers, the word 'Lord' is actually set out in capitals: Lord. This signifies the unique and untranslatable name of God, sometimes rendered as 'Jehovah' and particularly associated with God's relationship with Israel through the covenant made with Abraham (see Genesis 15). In declaring this blessing over the people, Aaron and his sons will 'put the name' – that inexpressibly holy name – upon them, as if enfolding them with a mantle of protection.

Listen to a recording of the composer John Rutter's arrangement of this blessing, 'The Lord Bless You and Keep You'. Pray that the words may be made real in your life today.

NAOMI STARKEY

Wednesday 14 May — **Numbers 9:15–18 (NRSV)**

Cloud and fire

On the day the tabernacle was set up, the cloud covered the tabernacle, the tent of the covenant, and from evening until morning it was over the tabernacle, having the appearance of fire. It was always so: the cloud covered it by day and the appearance of fire by night. Whenever the cloud lifted from over the tent, then the Israelites would set out, and in the place where the cloud settled down, there the Israelites would camp. At the command of the Lord the Israelites would set out, and at the command of the Lord they would camp. As long as the cloud rested over the tabernacle, they would remain in camp.

In the Bible, cloud and smoke were associated with God's presence or appearance (a 'theophany', to use the theological term). The cloud in our passage today, with 'the appearance of fire' by night, has a similar symbolism to the cloud on Mount Sinai when God gives Moses the law (Exodus 24). It is also a reminder of the 'smoke' filling the temple when Isaiah received his calling (Isaiah 6). In the New Testament, Jesus ascends to the Father, hidden by a cloud (Acts 1:9), and it is said that he will come again 'with the clouds' (Revelation 1:7).

The years in the wilderness may have been full of hardships but they were later viewed as a time of special closeness between God and his people. Led through the desert by that cloud of presence, the Israelites were humbled, tested and brought to realise how much they needed God's care and mercy. Such lessons were forgotten all too quickly when they finally entered Canaan.

Personal 'wilderness times' can be demanding and draining in the extreme – yet they can also be times when we learn what it means to be totally dependent on God. When we know we cannot take another step alone, we can discover a 'peace beyond understanding' in leaning on our heavenly Father. The challenge is then to continue our commitment to that closeness when the dark days are past.

---

*'Let the fiery cloudy pillar lead me all my journey through;
strong deliverer, be thou still my strength and shield'
(William Williams Pantycelyn, 1717–91).*

NAOMI STARKEY

Thursday 15 May — **Numbers 11:4–8 (NRSV, abridged)**

Bread of heaven

The camp followers with them had a strong craving, and the Israelites also wept again and said, 'If only we had meat to eat! We remember the fish we used to eat in Egypt for nothing, the cucumbers, the melons, the leeks, the onions, and the garlic, but now our strength is dried up, and there is nothing at all but this manna to look at.' Now the manna was like coriander seed, and its colour was like the colour of gum resin. The people… gathered it, ground it in mills or beat it in mortars, then boiled it in pots and made cakes of it; and the taste of it was like… cakes baked with oil.

After the details of national census and liturgical practice, the mouth-watering descriptions of food here bring a vivid human touch to the narrative. We can picture the Israelites lamenting together, talking (as hungry people do) about what they 'used to eat' in Egypt, apparently forgetting their former slave status. The dry desert landscape, bereft of green and growing things, would have been a further reminder of what they were missing.

There is also another attempt to describe the miraculous food provided by God: in Hebrew 'manna', meaning 'What is it?', is first mentioned in Exodus 16. The way that manna was to be gathered and stored was subject to strict laws, and although it sounds tasty – 'like wafers made with honey' (Exodus 16:31) – the Israelites had clearly lost their appetite for it after nearly two years. It was not just 'the rabble' (a reference to the non-Israelites travelling with them) who were literally fed up with the dietary situation.

There is a sad inevitability about miracles starting to seem commonplace and becoming taken for granted. Admittedly, it is hard to sustain a sense of wonder about something that happens every day, but it can be spiritually refreshing to pause and notice, once again, God's provision in our lives. That provision may not be 'miraculous', overturning the normal patterns of nature, but especially if it comes as an answer to prayer, we will be blessed in noticing it and being thankful.

Saying grace before meals tends to be a childhood practice. How might it benefit us in adult life?

NAOMI STARKEY

Friday 16 May — **Numbers 11:10–14 (NRSV, abridged)**

The weight of leadership

Moses heard the people weeping… at the entrances of their tents. Then the Lord became very angry, and Moses was displeased. So Moses said to the Lord… 'Why have I not found favour in your sight, that you lay the burden of all this people on me? Did I conceive all this people? Did I give birth to them, that you should say to me, "Carry them in your bosom as a wet nurse carries a nursing child, to the land that you promised on oath to their ancestors"? Where am I to get meat to give to all this people?… I am not able to carry all this people alone, for they are too heavy for me.'

At the start of this chapter, the people 'complained about their misfortunes' and the 'fire of the Lord burned against them' (Numbers 11:1). Then, Moses pleaded for mercy; now, Moses has had enough. In a chain reaction of despair, the sound of their weeping drives him to an outburst shocking in its honesty. He rages at God for seemingly setting him up to fail. Far from being the honoured leader at the head of a nation, he feels like a babysitter, burdened with a grumpy toddler.

We might have expected the 'fire of the Lord' to burn against him, too. Instead, God instructs him to appoint 70 elders to receive a spiritual anointing so that they can assist him (vv. 16–30). The hungry Israelites are punished for their rebellion by a surfeit of the meat they had longed for (vv. 18–20) and then a deadly plague strikes down those 'who had the craving' (v. 34).

Can we pray – even rage – as honestly as Moses did? Or should we tiptoe around, fearing a thunderbolt if we breathe a word of discontent? We must hold on to the love and mercy of God, as revealed to us supremely in the death of God's only Son. The danger of immersing ourselves in lament, as the Israelites did, is that it can lock us away from reaching out for the very love and mercy we so badly need.

Hold before God those whom you know in church leadership. Pray for God to bless them with wisdom, courage, energy and kindness.

NAOMI STARKEY

Saturday 17 May — **Numbers 12:1–5 (NRSV, abridged)**

Family feuding

While they were at Hazeroth, Miriam and Aaron spoke against Moses because of the Cushite woman whom he had married… and they said, 'Has the Lord spoken only through Moses? Has he not spoken through us also?' And the Lord heard it. Now the man Moses was very humble, more so than anyone else on the face of the earth. Suddenly the Lord said to Moses, Aaron, and Miriam, 'Come out, you three, to the tent of meeting.' So the three of them came out. Then the Lord came down in a pillar of cloud and stood at the entrance of the tent and called Aaron and Miriam, and they both came forward.

This dramatic moment brings to mind the Lord calling out Adam and Eve after they had eaten the forbidden fruit (Genesis 3). Moses' brother and sister have turned against him partly because of his choice of wife ('Cushite' implies 'Ethiopian') and partly because they are, simply, jealous. The Lord hears them; the Lord summons them; the Lord judges them. When the cloud of God's presence departs after the brother and sister's encounter with the Lord, Miriam's skin has become 'diseased, as white as snow' (v. 10). Thankfully, after Moses pleads for healing, she is restored after a seven-day exile.

We can draw a number of lessons from this story: respect your leaders; family disputes are nothing new; punishment should be followed by restoration. This last point is always in danger of being forgotten, especially when the deed punished involves some kind of sexual misdemeanour. Of course, justice must be done (and seen to be done, as it was in the case of Miriam). Justice should not, however, remove the possibility of an eventual way back from disgrace. Returning to the scene and situation of a 'fall' will probably not be right or possible – but if we worship a God of forgiveness, we cannot act as if some sins (those breaking the code of the church rather than the law of the land) are totally and forever beyond redemption.

Think of a situation where somebody – especially somebody in leadership – has fallen from grace. What might restoration look like, taking into account the need to balance mercy with justice?

NAOMI STARKEY

Sunday 18 May   **Numbers 13:27–30 (NRSV)**

Reality check

[The spies] reported to [Moses] and said, 'We came to the land to which you sent us; it flows with milk and honey, and this is its fruit. Yet the people who live in the land are strong, and the towns are fortified and very large, and besides, we saw the descendants of Anak there. The Amalekites live in the land of the Negeb; the Hittites, the Jebusites, and the Amorites live in the hill country, and the Canaanites live by the sea and along the Jordan.' But Caleb quieted the people before Moses and said, 'Let us go up at once and occupy it, for we are well able to overcome it.'

The journey is nearly over. The people are encamped on the borders of Canaan, and God orders Moses to send twelve men to spy out the land, one from each of the tribes. After a lengthy trip they return with eyewitness reports and a bunch of grapes – 'This is its fruit' (v. 27) – so large that it takes two men to carry it on a pole (v. 23).

Unfortunately, this is not only a land of milk, honey and giant grapes. Canaan is already populated with formidable settlements and even more formidable people: 'To ourselves we seemed like grasshoppers, and so we seemed to them' (v. 33). Of the twelve explorers, only Caleb and Joshua continue to trust that the Lord who has led them thus far will also lead them into the promised land. The book of Joshua tells how the conquest finally happened years later, but despite much looting, burning and death, a significant non-Israelite population survived to live alongside the conquerors.

It is impossible to read the list of resident tribes and not think of the ongoing conflicts in that very same region, centred on the issues of land ownership and belonging. The questions raised by the whole promised land narrative are too big to answer here. We must hold on to them, though, because the struggle to understand 'why' can help us shape a braver, more resilient faith that is unafraid to admit that we do not understand.

Pray for all who labour for peace in the Holy Land,
so many of them unseen and unthanked.

NAOMI STARKEY

The Fifth Sunday of Easter

Monday 19 May   **Numbers 14:20, 22–25 (NRSV, abridged)**

Back-tracking

Then the Lord said… 'None of the people who have seen my glory and the signs that I did in Egypt and in the wilderness and yet have tested me these ten times and have not obeyed my voice shall see the land that I swore to give to their ancestors… But my servant Caleb, because he has a different spirit and has followed me wholeheartedly, I will bring into the land into which he went, and his descendants shall possess it. Now, since the Amalekites and the Canaanites live in the valleys, turn tomorrow and set out for the wilderness by the way to the Red Sea.'

The spies' report of Canaan as 'a land that devours its inhabitants' (13:32) results, predictably, in mass rebellion. The people's furious attacks on Moses and Aaron include a plan to 'choose a captain and go back to Egypt' (14:4). Caleb and Joshua's pleas to hold on to the original vision of entering the land – because 'the Lord is with us' (v. 9) lead to threats of death by stoning. The Lord speaks of casting off the people forever and making Moses the founding father of a new nation.

Moses begs eloquently for mercy and, finally, the Lord relents – but at a price. Instead of entering their promised inheritance, God's people must now return to the desert places. They must go back to manna and wandering and wilderness life until the next generation is ready for what their parents were too fearful to do: 'Your little ones, who you said would become plunder… shall know the land that you have despised' (v. 31).

Despite Caleb and Joshua's loyalty to the Lord, they still suffer the same fate. Although they will both live long enough to enter Canaan eventually, there are no shortcuts for them. They will have to return to the wilderness too. We tend to assume that standing up for truth and obedience will automatically bring reward; this is a reminder that any such reward may be a long time in coming.

Pray for courage for those preparing to speak out against wrongdoing and injustice, especially when the decision will come at personal cost.

NAOMI STARKEY

Tuesday 20 May   **Numbers 16:41–46 (NRSV, abridged)**

Standing in the gap

The whole congregation of the Israelites rebelled against Moses and against Aaron, saying, 'You have killed the people of the Lord.' And when the congregation had assembled against them, Moses and Aaron turned towards the tent of meeting; the cloud had covered it, and the glory of the Lord appeared… And the Lord spoke to Moses, saying, 'Get away from this congregation, so that I may consume them in a moment'… Moses said to Aaron, 'Take your censer, put fire on it from the altar and lay incense on it and carry it quickly to the congregation and make atonement for them. For wrath has gone out from the Lord; the plague has begun.'

The waves of rebellion continue after the turning away from Canaan. After a failed invasion (attempted without Moses or the ark of the covenant, representing God's presence), a group from the tribes of Levi and Reuben challenge Moses' authority – with fatal results (vv. 31–35). That is the point at which our reading begins: the 'whole congregation of the Israelites' accuse both Moses and Aaron of killing 'the people of the Lord' (the rebels and their families). As the Lord's glory manifests at the tent of meeting and plague starts spreading through the camp, it feels as if the whole Exodus story is coming to a catastrophic end.

Then, instead of directly begging for mercy, Moses directs his brother, the high priest, to make a dramatic intervention. Burning incense, an ancient symbol of prayer rising to God, Aaron stands 'between the dead and the living' (v. 48) to 'make atonement' for the people's sins. The plague stops; many have died but many more are now spared.

Aaron's action feels like a faint foreshadowing of the atoning death of Jesus, a deep truth echoing through time that an innocent person, offering themselves freely, can somehow take away the guilt of others. He had not rebelled (not this time); he was willing to put himself in the most dangerous position of all and that was enough to halt the retribution. The price of sin had been paid; the wilderness wanderings could begin again.

What is the significance of apologies made for historic wrongdoing, even when the original perpetrators are long gone?

NAOMI STARKEY

Wednesday 21 May   **Numbers 20:10–13 (NRSV)**

Place of quarrelling

Moses and Aaron gathered the assembly together before the rock, and he said to them, 'Listen, you rebels; shall we bring water for you out of this rock?' Then Moses lifted up his hand and struck the rock twice with his staff; water came out abundantly, and the congregation and their livestock drank. But the Lord said to Moses and Aaron, 'Because you did not trust in me, to show my holiness before the eyes of the Israelites, therefore you shall not bring this assembly into the land that I have given them.' These are the waters of Meribah, where the Israelites quarrelled with the Lord and through which he showed himself to be holy.

This is the episode referenced at the end of Psalm 95, which is part of the Anglican service of Morning Prayer. Modern versions of the liturgy suggest omitting those verses because of their sombre note: 'Do not harden your hearts, as at Meribah' (Psalm 95:8). The contrast is felt to be too stark to the joyful opening: 'O come, let us sing to the Lord.'

While commending the desire not to upset congregations (nor put off newcomers), I prefer the full *Venite* (the psalm's ancient name, from the Latin for 'O come') because of its sobering reminder of human waywardness. Although the Lord is 'the rock of our salvation' (Psalm 95:1), we may still refuse to heed his voice just as the Israelites refused. Shockingly, even Moses falls short here, striking – instead of ordering – the rock to produce water for the people.

It is hard to see why this deed is so terrible that neither Moses nor Aaron is allowed to complete the journey to Canaan. Perhaps we find a clue in Moses' words: 'Shall we bring water for you out of this rock?' (v. 10). Perhaps he has forgotten how it was his long-ago desert encounter with the Lord (Exodus 3) that changed him from fumbling, frightened fugitive, 'slow of tongue' (Exodus 4:10), to prophetic leader. Infected with the people's anger, he is now infected with their desire for control as well, assuming the power that belongs to God alone.

'If you think you are standing, watch out that you do not fall'
(1 Corinthians 10:12).

NAOMI STARKEY

Thursday 22 May   **Numbers 21:5–9 (NRSV, abridged)**

Testing times

The people spoke against God and against Moses, 'Why have you brought us up out of Egypt to die in the wilderness?'… Then the Lord sent poisonous serpents among the people, and they bit the people, so that many Israelites died. The people came to Moses and said, 'We have sinned by speaking against the Lord and against you; pray to the Lord to take away the serpents from us.' So Moses prayed for the people. And the Lord said to Moses, 'Make a poisonous serpent, and set it on a pole, and everyone who is bitten shall look at it and live.' So Moses made a serpent of bronze and put it upon a pole, and whenever a serpent bit someone, that person would look at the serpent of bronze and live.

Again the people beg to know 'why', forgetting the answers they may have already received. Why were they brought out of Egypt? Why are they stuck in the desert? Why is there nothing good to eat or drink? When times are hard, it is difficult to maintain true perspective and even more difficult to take the long view. Even if exasperating, the complaints are understandable and raise a justifiable question of their own: 'Why does God respond with poisonous serpents?'

This is another hard passage, which demands that we hold in tension different truths because of the absence of easy answers. It is true that the Lord is full of mercy, grace and steadfast love (Exodus 34:6); it is true that trusting in the Lord is always better than relying on your own insight (Proverbs 3:5); it is true that sins are forgiven even if the damaging consequences of sin endure.

We can also hold on to the conclusion of the story: all the people have to do is look at the bronze serpent and then they will live. Deliverance is as easy as that; salvation is as simple as a trusting gaze in the right direction, as the thief on the cross discovered, centuries later (see Luke 23:42).

'Just as Moses lifted up the serpent in the wilderness, so must the Son of Man be lifted up, that whoever believes in him may have eternal life'
(John 3:14–15).

NAOMI STARKEY

Friday 23 May   **Numbers 22:1, 4–6, 21 (NRSV, abridged)**

Don't forget the donkey

The Israelites set out, and camped in the plains of Moab… Now Balak son of Zippor was king of Moab at that time. He sent messengers to Balaam son of Beor… saying, 'A people has come out of Egypt; they have spread over the face of the earth, and they have settled next to me. Come now, curse this people for me, since they are stronger than I; perhaps I shall be able to defeat them and drive them from the land, for I know that whomever you bless is blessed, and whomever you curse is cursed'… So Balaam got up in the morning, saddled his donkey, and went with the officials of Moab.

Today's passage is the start of a story that stretches across three chapters, with four prophetic oracles – and, of course, one talking donkey. One of the kings in the region of Canaan, finding a new nation encamped in his lands, sends for a prophet to curse them. Although Balaam is not an Israelite (hailing from the modern-day border area of Turkey and Syria), he is clearly guided by God (v. 8) in his task of divination. Unsurprisingly, despite repeated attempts, he is unable to curse God's people but instead speaks an impressive series of blessings.

On their way to meet the king, Balaam and his party are halted by the 'angel of the Lord' (v. 22), whom only Balaam's donkey can see. Balaam beats the donkey for halting until God grants the poor creature the temporary gift of speech (I assume it was temporary) to rebuke its master. The prophet then sees the spiritual adversary on the road ahead 'with his drawn sword in his hand' (v. 31). An animal's instinct has saved its owner's life, as has happened on countless other occasions since.

As well as the donkey, the story of Balaam the prophet and Balak the king is notable for two other reasons: the way God chooses to act through someone who is not one of God's people; the way God's purposes cannot be thwarted, no matter how impressive the human and spiritual forces ranged against them.

'What then are we to say about these things?
If God is for us, who is against us?' (Romans 8:31).

NAOMI STARKEY

Saturday 24 May — **Numbers 27:15–20 (NRSV)**

Succession planning

Moses spoke to the Lord, saying, 'Let the Lord, the God of the spirits of all flesh, appoint someone over the congregation who shall go out before them and come in before them, who shall lead them out and bring them in, so that the congregation of the Lord may not be like sheep without a shepherd.' So the Lord said to Moses, 'Take Joshua son of Nun, a man in whom is the spirit, and lay your hand upon him; have him stand before Eleazar the priest and all the congregation and commission him in their sight. You shall give him some of your authority, so that all the congregation of the Israelites may obey.'

As already mentioned, the Bible often presents time in the wilderness as a time of learning as well as testing. It may be a time of preparation, as in Jesus' time in the wilderness after his baptism (Matthew 4:1). It may also be a time for learning to rely on God, as Elijah discovers after defeating the priests of Baal (1 Kings 19:4). During their sojourn in the wilderness, the Israelites experience much testing and learning as they prepare for the long-delayed entry into their new homeland.

The task of leadership must pass on from Moses, though, because of his own rebellion (see 21 May). Joshua was one of the two spies who continued to trust that God would help them enter Canaan. It will be Joshua, and not Moses, who finally completes the Exodus journey.

The death of Moses is not mentioned until the very end of Deuteronomy. Appointing Joshua did not mean that Moses' work had finished, but he knew the importance of showing that his care for his nation involved planning for the time after his departure; sheep always need a shepherd. The story of the people of Israel would not end with the final breath of their great leader.

Pray for any church leaders you know who are moving to a new ministry (whether another paid role or retirement). Pray that they may have courage to step forward into the future and faith to entrust to God's care the people they leave behind.

NAOMI STARKEY

Introduction

Luke 13—16

Over the next two weeks we will explore some familiar parables, healing miracles and life guidance from Jesus. Two questions may come to mind as we journey, possibly questions that challenge us in new ways.

First, how good are we at waiting? Waiting seems to be a dying art in our society. We have been encouraged to buy what we want and think about paying for it later. Patience does not come easily. Our reflections begin with an example of patience, as a gardener pleads for more time to give a failing fig tree another chance to bear fruit.

The natural world is more patient. The mustard seed needs years to become the tree in which the birds can build their nests, and it takes time for the yeast to work its magic when mixed with the flour. Human patience is also in evidence, however, in the father of the prodigal son, who waits for years, never giving up hope of seeing his lost son again, and welcoming him home with open arms when he returns, broken and remorseful.

Woven into this theme of waiting is the second question: how do we learn to let go of the things we cling to? Even the yeast has to let go of its yeast-nature if it is to fulfil its role in making bread, and the mustard seed has to die before it can grow into a tree. Jesus warns us that we must enter through a narrow door, which means leaving all our baggage behind.

Baggage comes in many different forms. Perhaps we cling to our status, like the guest who takes a place of honour at the banquet, or to our right to choose as our table companions those who are likely to return the invitation. Or perhaps, like the prodigal son, we cling to our determination to do things our own way, or his elder brother who clings to his sense of self-righteous entitlement.

During these two weeks we also celebrate Ascension Day, when Jesus let go of his earthly presence. His friends, in their turn, had to let him go. The letting go is followed by Jesus' invitation to wait for the coming of the Holy Spirit.

Letting go, waiting, trusting. These are the themes of our journey during these weeks.

MARGARET SILF

Sunday 25 May   **Luke 13:6–9 (NRSV)**

The God of second chances

Then he told this parable: 'A man had a fig tree planted in his vineyard, and he came looking for fruit on it and found none. So he said to the man working the vineyard, "See here! For three years I have come looking for fruit on this fig tree, and still I find none. Cut it down! Why should it be wasting the soil?" He replied, "Sir, let it alone for one more year, until I dig round it and put manure on it. If it bears fruit next year, well and good, but if not, you can cut it down."'

This story might fill us with trepidation. What if I am a fig tree like that, a disappointment to the one who planted me, because I am failing to bear fruit? Most of us are more likely to be painfully aware of our failures than our achievements. So do we perhaps see 'God' like this – a vineyard owner coming to look for the fruits that he has every right to expect from his trees? Do we deserve to be cut down and condemned as a waste of space?

We might first ponder the question: what fruit are we being asked to bear? Here the response might well differ from the world's view of fruitfulness. A list of achievements might impress the world, but carry no weight with the divine vintner, who is looking for the fruits of love, kindness, patience, tolerance and a willingness to put the needs of our neighbour before our own. If our lives lack these fruits, then we are spiritually barren.

The gardener, knowing our weakness, pleads our case, asking the vineyard owner for more time to work on us and with us. The second chance that the parable offers involves work and discomfort. To grow in love requires us to ask, in our everyday life situations, 'What is the more loving way to respond? What is love asking of me here?' These promptings are like the prongs of the fork digging around our hearts or the dung that will encourage us to grow.

There is still time to become more fruitful, but not an endless supply of it. Our lives are short, and the harvest of love is desperately needed in our troubled world.

MARGARET SILF

The Sixth Sunday of Easter

Monday 26 May   **Luke 13:10–13 (NRSV)**

Walking tall

Now he was teaching in one of the synagogues on the Sabbath. And just then there appeared a woman with a spirit that had crippled her for eighteen years. She was bent over and was quite unable to stand up straight. When Jesus saw her, he called her over and said, 'Woman, you are set free from your ailment.' When he laid his hands on her, immediately she stood straight and began praising God.

It had been a long time since I last saw my old school friend. Our lives had gone down different paths, and I had moved to a distant part of the country and lost touch with her. The years passed, and several decades later I moved back to our old childhood neighbourhood.

I knew that the years would have taken their toll on both of us, but it still came as a shock when I spotted her walking down the road. The young girl I had once known as a classmate, a fellow hiker and a trusted confidante had become a bent old woman, making her way tentatively step by painful step. What could have happened in her life to cripple her so?

This incident comes to mind when I reflect on the event described in today's reading. Jesus healed the crippled woman in a moment, instantly recognising the burden that was weighing her down. Such miracles take a great deal longer in human time, but perhaps they are no less a sign of God's healing love at work.

It was a long time before my old friend opened up about the intervening years and the troubles that oppressed her. Jesus' healing touch is instantaneous. My friend's healing needed a long time and a supportive community of friends and neighbours. Now when I see her walking along the road there is a spring in her step. She walks tall again, free once more to be the person God created her to be. They say it takes a village to raise a child. Sometimes it takes a village to help free a troubled soul from what oppresses her.

Sometimes we are called to participate in God's healing action. Perhaps you know someone who is bent over in fear or sorrow or loneliness?

MARGARET SILF

Tuesday 27 May   **Luke 13:18–21 (NRSV)**

Surrender to a greater purpose

He said therefore, 'What is the kingdom of God like? And to what should I compare it? It is like a mustard seed that someone took and sowed in the garden; it grew and became a tree, and the birds of the air made nests in its branches.' And again he said, 'To what should I compare the kingdom of God? It is like yeast that a woman took and mixed in with three measures of flour until all of it was leavened.'

Today we reflect on two parables, each with an encouraging promise but also with a challenge. First we have the very familiar comparison of the kingdom of God with a mustard seed so small that you can hold it between your fingers, yet able to grow into a tree so great that the birds can build their nests in it. This assures us that however small we are, however apparently trivial our contribution, the little we can bring to the service of the kingdom will grow, by God's grace, into more than we can possibly imagine, giving life to the world.

The second parable compares the kingdom to a small amount of yeast, which alone can do nothing, but when mixed with the flour will provide a loaf for the nourishing of many. This is another encouraging promise that the tiny contribution we feel able to make to the coming of God's reign is essential to the process of bringing more and more fulness of life to the world.

These are the encouragements. The challenge lies in the fact that these miracles can only happen if we are willing to let go of what we think we can achieve independently in our own strength and to surrender our deepest selves to a greater purpose. The mustard seed will only bring forth the tree if it is first buried in the ground. The yeast will only make possible the baking of life-giving bread if it is willing to surrender its yeast-nature and allow itself to be mixed with the flour. The bringing forth of the newness of life depends on the letting go of the old.

We are called to become more than we imagine possible,
but only when we let go of our lesser selves.

MARGARET SILF

Wednesday 28 May   **Luke 13:24–27a (NRSV)**

The narrow door

'Strive to enter through the narrow door, for many, I tell you, will try to enter and will not be able. Once the owner of the house has got up and shut the door, and you begin to stand outside and to knock at the door, saying "Lord, open to us", then in reply he will say to you, "I do not know where you come from." Then you will begin to say, "We ate and drank with you, and you taught in our streets." But he will say, "I do not know where you come from."'

There is a peak in the English Lake District called Napes Needle. It gets this name because it is a pinnacle at the summit of Great Gable with a very distinctive narrow gap, like the eye of a needle. Climbers who manage to reach the summit and get through its rocky 'eye' call it 'threading the needle'. Today's reading reminds me of this challenging ascent.

    Jesus speaks of a narrow door. No doubt many climbers aspiring to 'thread' Napes Needle fail to do so. Those who succeed are those who realise that they must first leave behind their backpacks. You cannot get through the eye of the needle if you are carrying anything other than yourself. You cannot get through the narrow door if you are loaded with baggage.

    Perhaps we are invited today to reflect on the nature of any baggage blocking our way through the narrow door. Is there something that we cling to and refuse to let go? Are we holding on to old hurts or resentments or refusing to forgive those who have harmed us?

    Or do we think that because we have kept the rules and carried out our religious duties this opens the door for us? If so, Jesus goes on to warn us that it is not so much about going through the right motions and listening to the right teaching. It is about seeking to know him more clearly and follow him more closely, so that we become more like him.

May we have the grace to let ourselves come closer to God in our innermost hearts. Then the door will be opened, and we will hear the welcome: 'Come on in.'

MARGARET SILF

Thursday 29 May   **Luke 24:48–53 (NRSV)**

Don't cling

'You are witnesses of these things. And see, I am sending upon you what my Father promised, so stay here in the city until you have been clothed with power from on high.' Then he led them out as far as Bethany, and, lifting up his hands, he blessed them. While he was blessing them, he withdrew from them and was carried up into heaven. And they worshipped him and returned to Jerusalem with great joy, and they were continually in the temple blessing God.

Our journey so far with Luke has raised questions about letting go and about waiting for the working of grace in God's time, not our own. Today, on Ascension Day, these themes are especially apparent.

    I once learned something about letting go during a residential work course. Quite unexpectedly it had been a time when God seemed very close. On my last day there I walked around the grounds, wishing that I could hold on to this time of spiritual consolation for ever. I did not want to leave. Perhaps these thoughts became prayers, because it felt as though a response was stirring in my heart that I felt could only be coming from God. It seemed to be telling me: 'Don't cling to what you have been given here for it is already lodged forever in your heart. Move on with empty hands, because I have so much more to give. You can only receive this if your hands are empty. Let go of the "less", however good it is, to make space for the "more".'

    I have never forgotten those special days, and the promise of the 'more' has been fulfilled. I only had to wait, with empty hands. Perhaps it was a bit like this for those first friends of Jesus who witnessed his dramatic departure and also bore witness to the fulfilment of the promise of so much more to come. They too had to let go of the relationship of daily contact they had enjoyed with Jesus, wonderful though this had been, and wait patiently for the even greater gift of the Holy Spirit.

May we have the grace to let go of all that has been in order to receive all that is still to come.

MARGARET SILF

Friday 30 May   Luke 13:34–35 (NRSV)

The cost of rejection

'Jerusalem, Jerusalem, the city that kills the prophets and stones those who are sent to it! How often have I desired to gather your children together as a hen gathers her brood under her wings, and you were not willing! See, your house is left to you. And I tell you, you will not see me until the time comes when you say, "Blessed is the one who comes in the name of the Lord."'

When I think of this incident and Jesus' heart-rending words, I cannot help thinking of how an adolescent tantrum might look. A mother at the end of her tether thinks of how often she has gathered her children in her arms, tried to lead them in the ways of goodness and truth, protected them from harm and enfolded them in her love. Yet they rejected her guidance. They defied her and went their own stubborn ways.

Adolescent rejection is usually a passing, if deeply painful, phase, but here Jesus recognises something more lasting and more deadly. He compares the rejection of his message to the history of how Jerusalem (implying God's people) has attacked and killed those who came with an invitation of salvation. Today he would recognise the same pattern in the human family everywhere, reacting with sometimes violent opposition when our sinful ways are challenged, and refusing to be gathered as one family under one loving God.

More than one desperate parent will have told a rebellious brood: 'Okay, if that's how you want it, go your own ways and see how you fare.' When we reject the gathering of the loving parent, we will find that our place in the world becomes empty and desolate, just as Jesus warns the people that their temple will become desolate. We will only discover the magnitude of our loss when we repent and turn again to the one who comes in the name of the Lord.

Later in these reflections we will meet a vivid example of a son who decides he can do better on his own and lives to see the error of his ways.

Protect us from ourselves, we pray, and keep gathering, forgiving and blessing us, so that our lives too may be lived in the name of the Lord. Amen.

MARGARET SILF

Saturday 31 May — Luke 14:8–9, 11 (NRSV)

The dangers of entitlement

'When you are invited by someone to a wedding banquet, do not sit down at the place of honour, in case someone more distinguished than you has been invited by your host, and the host who invited both of you may come and say to you, "Give this person your place", and then in disgrace you would start to take the lowest place… For all who exalt themselves will be humbled, and those who humble themselves will be exalted.'

We were probably taught as children that it was bad behaviour 'to blow our own trumpet'. I am not musically gifted myself, but I deeply respect and admire the discipline involved in playing in an orchestra. Imagine if one player decides to play so loudly that the whole ensemble is spoiled and the contribution of the other players drowned out. Eventually the conductor has to ask the rogue player to stand down.

Today's reading places this problem in the context of a banquet. The focus is all on the guest who thinks he is entitled to a place of honour and risks being asked to move to a lower place. His arrogance switches the focus away from the wedding gathering and on to himself.

Wherever such shows of entitlement happen, Jesus urges us to practise appropriate humility and recognise that we are part of something much greater than ourselves. He warns us of what happens when we push ourselves forward, claiming rights and status for ourselves and valuing our own importance more highly than that of others. He is uncompromising in his comments about this kind of behaviour. Those who put themselves forward will be brought low and those who display humility, putting the common good above their own, will be invited to come forward.

If we take this teaching to heart we might notice that the people most qualified to be leaders in society are actually those who least desire the status. Two recent British monarchs, for example, never wanted or expected to wear the crown, but became humble, trusted and much cherished guides to their people.

When we put ourselves forward, we block the light for others. When we put the common good before our own, we make space for the light to shine on all.

MARGARET SILF

Sunday 1 June   **Luke 14:12b–14 (NRSV)**

A different kind of guest list

'When you give a luncheon or a dinner, do not invite your friends or your brothers and sisters or your relatives or rich neighbours, in case they may invite you in return, and you would be repaid. But when you give a banquet, invite the poor, the crippled, the lame, and the blind. And you will be blessed because they cannot repay you, for you will be repaid at the resurrection of the righteous.'

I am reminded of a moving episode in the British television series *Downton Abbey* in which some of the servants are enjoying a picnic together after two of them have just finished taking an exam. They are a motley group. They had no chance to choose their companions. Their work has just thrown them together and they have to see how they get along. It is hardly a banquet, but they are enjoying each other's company even though they did not choose it.

They discuss one of the exam papers, and then someone passes the paper to one young man in the group and asks him to read the first question out loud. There is an awkward silence. The young man stumbles over the first few words and then looks around the group and admits that he cannot read. He feels ashamed and wishes he could just disappear. The others are surprised, but sympathetic about this revelation, but one of them, who has had some teaching experience, immediately offers to teach him to read.

Upstairs in the big house the family have careful discussions about who to invite to their formal dinners. Kindly though they are, they expect to select their guests and thus control whose company they keep. There will be no invitation to the illiterate or disadvantaged. And inevitably there will be the social expectation of return hospitality in due course.

Jesus, I believe, would have thoroughly enjoyed the servants' picnic and would have gratefully embraced the teacher who reached out in love to help the embarrassed young man. To the family upstairs he might well have directed today's warning, but he would have done so in love.

Miracles can happen when we let go of our control over our guest lists and allow the unexpected to surprise us.

MARGARET SILF

Monday 2 June   **Luke 14:27–28, 33–35 (NRSV)**

Counting the cost

'Whoever does not carry the cross and follow me cannot be my disciple. For which of you, intending to build a tower, does not first sit down and estimate the cost, to see whether he has enough to complete it?… So therefore, none of you can become my disciple if you do not give up all your possessions. Salt is good, but if salt has lost its taste, how can its saltiness be restored? It is useful neither for the soil nor for the manure pile; they throw it away. If you have ears to hear, then hear!'

There was once a famous acrobat who entertained the crowds by walking a high wire across a gorge, without a safety net. One day he appeared with a wheelbarrow and asked the crowds, 'Do you believe I can walk the high wire pushing this wheelbarrow?' 'Yes, yes,' they cried, full of enthusiasm. 'Of course, we believe you can do it.' 'Then who's going to get in the wheelbarrow?' he asked.

This story speaks to the heart of today's reading. Jesus' warnings are as shocking as the challenge from the acrobat. It is one thing to affirm our belief, but how far does our commitment really go? It is easy to talk the talk. Much harder to walk the walk. To 'carry the cross' is to get into the wheelbarrow and place our trust entirely in the one who calls us to follow him.

Jesus is a realist. He knows our fears and understands them, and he warns us to think carefully and to count the cost, lest we try to get out of the wheelbarrow halfway across the gorge. He goes on to warn us about the risk of becoming lukewarm in our following. Just as salt loses its flavour over time, so our commitment to the gospel can become bland and uninspiring. The fire that once burned in our hearts can cool to ashes if we neglect the need to stay close to the one we follow. If this feels daunting, let us remember that however far we may drift away from him, he will always stay close to us.

May we have the grace to walk the distance
with the one who calls, leads and guides us.

MARGARET SILF

Tuesday 3 June   **Luke 15:3–6 (NRSV)**

Finding the lost sheep

He told them this parable: 'Which one of you, having a hundred sheep and losing one of them, does not leave the ninety-nine in the wilderness and go after the one that is lost until he finds it? And when he has found it, he lays it on his shoulders and rejoices. And when he comes home, he calls together his friends and neighbours, saying to them, "Rejoice with me, for I have found my lost sheep."'

Paul is a flight paramedic, often called out on rescue missions to the Scottish highlands and islands. But when he is on a helicopter mission, he is not just Paul; he is everyone who takes care of others. He is one of a team of countless women and men, worldwide, who go out searching tirelessly for those in trouble, every day, year on year, generation after generation.

On one call-out he and his colleagues were summoned to a drowning accident off the west coast of Scotland. A family had got into difficulty while canoeing, and one of the casualties was a little girl the same age as Paul's own daughter. The team worked all night to save the child's life. She was too unstable to be airlifted to the nearest hospital on the mainland, so the rescue team called on off-duty clinicians to attend and arranged for sophisticated life-support equipment to be transported to the scene.

When Paul finally got home, he first hugged his own children. Then with tears in his eyes, he said, 'Today I was proud to be part of such a team. When we couldn't get the patient to the hospital, we took the hospital to the patient.' There was such great rejoicing over the one who was so nearly lost, but was found.

This parable is being lived out in our world every moment of every day, as people who care deeply move heaven and earth to bring others to safety. Some are highly trained, others are simply ordinary folk, going to extraordinary lengths for the love of others. Some work for our emergency services, others simply live in your street.

We give thanks for those who came looking for us when we felt lost ourselves, and to the one who inspired them.

MARGARET SILF

Wednesday 4 June   **Luke 15:8–10 (NRSV)**

Searching for God

'Or what woman having ten silver coins, if she loses one of them, does not light a lamp, sweep the house, and search carefully until she finds it? And when she has found it, she calls together her friends and neighbours, saying, "Rejoice with me, for I have found the coin that I had lost." Just so, I tell you, there is joy in the presence of the angels of God over one sinner who repents.'

Most of us will have been in this situation. We have lost something important and searched high and low for it. Such searches often disintegrate into panic. Successful searches invariably end in great rejoicing when we find the missing key, glasses or passport. Our jubilation at the outcome of our search reminds us how much more God rejoices whenever a lost one is found again.

This parable leads me to ponder the deeper searches that occupy our hearts and minds. Whatever beliefs they may outwardly express, most people are searching for something – or someone – that they cannot name or understand.

There was once, it is said, a small boy who one morning packed himself some sandwiches and told his mother he was going to the park to look for God. Lunchtime came and he stopped at a park bench for a rest. An older lady was already sitting on the bench, and the boy started to chat to her. Then he thought she might be hungry too, so he shared his sandwiches with her. When he got back home his mother asked him, 'Did you find God?' 'Oh yes,' he said. 'And she has a lovely smile.' The older lady was having supper later with her husband. 'Did you have a good day?' he asked. 'Oh yes,' she replied. 'I found God in the park.' 'Really?' he said. 'And what was God like?' 'Much younger than I expected,' she replied.

We may think we have 'lost' God, but whenever we meet kindness, generosity, compassion and love, then we have found God, and others will catch a glimpse of God when they meet these qualities in us.

The ancient chant assures us that 'Ubi caritas et amor, Deus ibi est' ('Where love and charity are found, there is God.') Where have you found God this week?

MARGARET SILF

Thursday 5 June   Luke 15:11–13, 17–19 (NRSV)

The prodigal son

Then Jesus said, 'There was a man who had two sons. The younger of them said to his father, "Father, give me the share of the wealth that will belong to me." So he divided his assets between them. A few days later the younger son gathered all he had and travelled to a distant region, and there he squandered his wealth in dissolute living… But when he came to his senses he said… "I will get up and go to my father, and I will say to him, 'Father, I have sinned against heaven and before you; I am no longer worthy to be called your son; treat me like one of your hired hands.'"'

Much of the theme of these two weeks has been about letting go, and about waiting. In today's and tomorrow's readings we meet one young man who could not wait and another who could not let go.

The younger son in this familiar story would find plenty of kindred spirits in our world today. He knows what he wants and he wants it now. He would feel quite at home with today's culture of 'buy now, pay later'. A friend told me about her little niece who was out shopping with her mother one day. She saw a doll that she badly wanted and asked her mother to buy it. Mum suggested adding the doll to her Santa wish list. The child looked at her mother in astonishment: 'But Mum, Santa knows that I need it *now*.'

Not so long ago it was an accepted reality that you had to save for anything you wanted. This required discipline and patience, and it was simply the way things were. Then came credit cards and suddenly it was normal to be in debt. The younger son is like the child in the toy shop: he wants everything *now*, but as soon as he has it, he squanders it. His reckless lifestyle takes him down the slippery slope to destitution.

The grace-filled turning point of the parable, however, is when the lost young man is at his lowest point and ready to turn back in a spirit of sorrow, pay the price and seek forgiveness.

Rock bottom can be the place where we find repentance and new beginnings.

MARGARET SILF

Friday 6 June   **Luke 15:25, 28–30 (NRSV)**

The prodigal's brother

'Now his elder son was in the field, and as he came and approached the house, he heard music and dancing… Then he became angry and refused to go in. His father came out and began to plead with him. But he answered his father, "Listen! For all these years I have been working like a slave for you, and I have never disobeyed your command, yet you have never given me even a young goat so that I might celebrate with my friends. But when this son of yours came back, who has devoured your assets with prostitutes, you killed the fatted calf for him!"'

While his younger brother is away squandering his inheritance, the elder son is continuing business as usual, working in their father's fields, doing their father's bidding, with no immediate reward. He is also simmering with silent resentment, and this furious outburst was probably inevitable.

He has proved himself good at waiting and expects to wait patiently for his share of the inheritance in the fulness of time. His problem is that he cannot let go of his anger and resentment. He cannot let go of his sense of entitlement. His righteous indignation over this perceived injustice is in sharp contrast to his father's overwhelming generosity.

The father is able both to wait and to let go. He waits patiently until his errant son is ready to come home, never knowing what has become of his boy or whether he will ever see him again. This is a painful patience. And then, when he gets that first glimpse of the prodigal's return, he is able to let go of any lingering negative feelings and simply rejoice that the son he thought was lost has been found. There is no recrimination, reckoning, lecturing or demand for restitution. Quite the opposite: he runs with open arms to greet the returning son.

The elder son finds this impossible to swallow. Will he let go of his resentment and truly hear his father's subsequent assurance: 'Son, you are always with me and all that is mine is yours' (v. 31)? Will *you* let go of your own ideas of justice and hear that assurance too?

Justice matters, but generosity and loving acceptance matter even more.

MARGARET SILF

Saturday 7 June   **Luke 16:10a, 11–13 (NRSV)**

Faithfulness begins with small things

'Whoever is faithful in a very little is faithful also in much… If, then, you have not been faithful with the dishonest wealth, who will entrust to you the true riches? And if you have not been faithful with what belongs to another, who will give you what is your own? No slave can serve two masters, for a slave will either hate the one and love the other or be devoted to the one and despise the other. You cannot serve God and wealth.'

We end our two-week journey with Jesus' own summing-up of how we should conduct our human affairs, and especially those involving money, leading to the uncompromising choice he lays before us: God or wealth. This is the ultimate challenge of letting go. The choice may sound easy. In practice it is extremely difficult to live up to such a high ideal.

Today's reading gives us some invaluable guidance on the matter of integrity. First, we learn that it begins with the small things. The person who is trustworthy in the small things of everyday life can be trusted with bigger things. It follows that someone who is dishonest in small things will be dishonest in bigger things. This alone provides sound guidance, for example, on how we choose our leaders as well as how we live our own lives.

But Jesus is talking here about greater treasure than that in our purses or bank accounts. If we cannot be trusted with the small matters of life, how can we be trusted with the eternal treasure that the kingdom of God affords? Earthly possessions can so easily become chains that bind us to earth and its material attractions. We become so deeply attached that we cannot see beyond the short horizon of material gain.

God calls us to the longer view. The passing attractions of possessions, power or status are like clouds that block the sunlight. We could read today's final warning like this: 'If you choose to put your energy into clinging to the passing clouds you will never know the power of the sun. Let go of the lesser things if you truly desire the greater.'

May we learn to be faithful in the small things.
Integrity in the big things will follow.

MARGARET SILF

Introduction

Numbered for God

A few weeks ago Naomi Starkey led us through the Old Testament book of Numbers and we were reminded of some of its content and significance. For the next fortnight I am going to take us through a different set of numbers: not the biblical book, but rather the numbers we find in the Bible. This will involve jumping about from Genesis to Revelation, because, perhaps unsurprisingly, we are going to do this in numerical order.

Numerology has fascinated so many ancient and modern cultures, and some people still attribute meaning to the ways in which things are numbered, or speak in terms of 'lucky', 'auspicious' or 'unlucky' numbers. The number 13 is considered unlucky in the west, so much so that some say as many as ten per cent of the US population has a fear of the number 13, and the more specific fear of Friday 13th (paraskevidekatriaphobia) results in significant financial losses as people avoid marrying, travelling or even working on those days (of which there are at least a couple a year).

Superstition and numbers have gone hand in hand for a long time. This is not necessarily a bad thing, and understanding how and when can yield healthy insight into biblical times and attitudes which informed leaders and peoples or influenced those who wrote about their exploits and encounters.

Perhaps more mundanely, we all live our lives surrounded, driven and even controlled by numbers, not least those displayed on our clocks. There is also the tradition, found in the folk hymn 'When the saints go marching in', of being 'numbered' with – that is counted among – the saints. Resonances with some of our readings this fortnight are found in the song.

So I hope a little foray into some biblical numbers will prove interesting and enlightening, not least for the stories to which they relate and our own desire to be numbered among the holy ones of God.

GORDON GILES

Sunday 8 June   **Ephesians 4:1b, 3–6 (NRSV)**

One God and Father

Walk in a manner worthy of the calling to which you have been called… making every effort to maintain the unity of the Spirit in the bond of peace: there is one body and one Spirit, just as you were called to the one hope of your calling, one Lord, one faith, one baptism, one God and Father of all, who is above all and through all and in all.

The Romans and Greeks worshipped multiple gods, and some African and Asian religions do the same, but the world from which Christian culture arose and developed dispensed with polytheism. Moses established monotheism in reaction to Egyptian polytheism; Babylonian and Assyrian idol worship (involving Baal and others) was resisted by the prophets during the period of exile.

By the first century, Jewish culture was living cheek by jowl with Roman polytheism and once the apostle Paul started travelling around Asia Minor there were Greek beliefs to challenge. 'Christendom' developed, discussing what it meant to be a Christian and debating the most complex aspect of Christian doctrine – the Trinity. Even so, the three in one of the Godhead is fundamentally based on the oneness of God: Trinity in unity. Simultaneously the people of God – you and me – are one, because we are united – made one – in and under God who is, in three persons, one.

This singularity of faith is the pinnacle of faith and faiths, the ultimate direction of all believing, which is that there is, and can only be, one God. This God and Father of our Lord Jesus Christ is the creator of everything, the architect of the Big Bang, the one who was before all things and in all things, not only then, but now and in what is to come. The Spirit of God is inevitably also singular and is the common breath which gives life, the thread of ongoing faith that saves and sustains us.

There is just one, not many, and even for those who do not believe, it is the one God in whom they do not believe, whose singular Spirit they deny, whose only Son they reject. So pervasive is the oneness of God that even those who do not believe take it for granted.

God, may we never take you for granted, but always recognise and worship you as Father, Son and Holy Spirit, one God, now and always. Amen.

GORDON GILES

Monday 9 June   **Genesis 6:19–20 (NRSV)**

Two by two

And of every living thing, of all flesh, you shall bring two of every kind into the ark, to keep them alive with you; they shall be male and female. Of the birds according to their kinds and of the animals according to their kinds, of every creeping thing of the ground according to its kind, two of every kind shall come in to you, to keep them alive.

Procreation is a marvellous thing. We often take it for granted or get coy about it. As the song by Cole Porter famously and wittily puts it, every animal, including birds, bees and 'educated fleas', they all do it. They have to.

Humour and embarrassment aside, without it we would not exist. Reproduction is not simply something that we – or two (male and female) animals – 'do' but rather a miraculous collaboration between the natural and the divine. 'Pro' means 'with': the creation of new life involves the two-by-two *and* God. Procreation is the process and mechanism built into the divinely created order by which life is continued and sustained.

Noah is instructed to load his ark with paired animals. It is both practically and divinely necessary, and right. Along with the couples of humans in Noah's family, these are sufficient to propagate their species. It is an orderly plan and it succeeds. In a reversal of the classic case of abandoning a ship to make for the safety of land, here the land is to be abandoned for the safety of a ship. This counterintuitive approach indicates the radical reversal that the flood represents – God the creator destroying most of creation because it has turned away from righteousness.

We associate God with salvation, not destruction, and thus this story has always been challenging. Perhaps grounded in a widely recognised event in prehistory, described by various middle-eastern cultures, it reminds us that God is in everything, including the destructive forces found in a free universe. As the rainbow demonstrates, God is also the one who even in judgement saves his people and finds a way through the storms of sin and judgement.

Storm and sex are divinely ordained, and God uses them both for the good of his people.

Spare us from judgement, Lord, that in Christ we may survive and flourish. Amen.

GORDON GILES

Tuesday 10 June   **John 2:18–22a (NRSV)**

Three days

The Jews then said to him, 'What sign can you show us for doing this?' Jesus answered them, 'Destroy this temple, and in three days I will raise it up.' The Jews then said, 'This temple has been under construction for forty-six years, and will you raise it up in three days?' But he was speaking of the temple of his body. After he was raised from the dead, his disciples remembered that he had said this.

Sometimes we say Jesus was raised *on* the third day, *after* three days or even three days *later*. Such statements are not the same numerically. We know that Jesus died on the cross as sunset approached on (Good) Friday. He was entombed swiftly. 'Early on the first day of the week, while it was still dark', the women found the tomb empty (John 20:1). That could have been as few as 36 hours later. Certainly not three days later and, by modern parlance, not really the 'third day'.

Some commentators have therefore suggested that the last supper took place on the Wednesday (1 April AD33, to be precise), the crucifixion on Thursday and the resurrection three days later on Easter Day. Alternatively, we might say that if Good Friday is the first day, then Holy Saturday the second, and so as Easter dawns it is the third day.

We should recall that from Genesis onwards, the 'third day' is the day of new life: vegetation on the third day of creation and humanity another three days later. God told Abraham to sacrifice his son Isaac: 'On the third day Abraham looked up and saw the place far away' (Genesis 22:4). Hosea uses the same imagery (6:1–2), and famously Jonah spends three days in the belly of the fish (Jonah 1:17).

Like the Jews in today's passage, we might take the 'three days' too literally, questioning the maths. They do not recognise the ancient allusions. For what is far more important is the truth buried in these interconnected triduums (sets of three days) – it is God's loving, merciful way to bring new life from death, new hope from despair on, after or within three days.

Heavenly Father, as you raised Christ on the third day,
raise me from the death of sin to resurrection life. Amen.

GORDON GILES

Wednesday 11 June **Revelation 6:2, 4–5, 7–8 (NRSV, abridged)**

Four horses

I looked, and there was a white horse! Its rider had a bow; a crown was given to him, and he came out conquering and to conquer... And out came another horse, bright red; its rider was permitted to take peace from the earth, so that people would slaughter one another, and he was given a great sword... And there was a black horse! Its rider held a pair of scales in his hand... When he broke the fourth seal, I heard the voice of the fourth living creature call out, 'Come!' I looked, and there was a pale green horse! Its rider's name was Death, and Hades followed with him; they were given authority over a fourth of the earth, to kill with sword, famine, and pestilence and by the wild animals of the earth.

The four horsemen of the apocalypse have entered popular culture, being depicted by Albrecht Dürer in 1498 and making regular appearances in art, poetry, novels and films ever since. Demis Roussos' band Aphrodite's Child wrote a song called 'The Four Horsemen' for their concept album *666* in 1972, based on this passage and popular with heavy metal groups since.

The horses signify death, famine, war and plague (or pestilence): an ageless list of woes. Some people have even, light-heartedly perhaps, suggested that Google, Facebook, Apple and Amazon are the four horsemen of technology, bringing doom and disaster to our world.

Today's passage resonates with Zechariah 6:1–8, in which four chariots appear. The first has red horses, the second has black, the third white, and the fourth, dappled horses. The colours in today's passage have meaning: white for conquest; red for bloodshed; black for famine; and then green for plague. These are graphic and vivid, technicolour images.

We can relate to them all. Wars, famine, violent death and even plague (pandemic) have featured in our lives personally and globally. The text is not prediction but prophecy – interpreting the times as they *are*, as well as will be (and ever were). These mounted warriors on coloured steeds show us our world, we are aware of them and wary of them. Only by and in Christ can they be faced down.

Lord Jesus, at your feet we lay the burdens of the world
and in you we place our hope and trust. Amen.

GORDON GILES

Thursday 12 June — John 6:8–11 (NRSV)

Five loaves

One of his disciples, Andrew, Simon Peter's brother, said to him, 'There is a boy here who has five barley loaves and two fish. But what are they among so many people?' Jesus said, 'Make the people sit down.' Now there was a great deal of grass in the place, so they sat down, about five thousand in all. Then Jesus took the loaves, and when he had given thanks he distributed them to those who were seated; so also the fish, as much as they wanted.

It is not a major feat of mathematics to work out that five loaves among 5,000 people is one loaf per thousand people: which is probably not measurable even in crumbs! They were not family-sized loaves either. The fish, which were likely sardines, had to go round even further – two and a half thousand people per fish. The maths of this mysterious multiplication is so marvellous that it must be considered a miracle.

There are five gold rings in the twelve days of Christmas, and five books of the Pentateuch (the ancient Hebrew law, which is still enshrined in Genesis–Deuteronomy). These collections of stories, rules and regulations were by no means meagre, and there was plenty to go around. In Jesus, however, the law reaches its culmination and, as the miracle of multiplication demonstrates, less is more. The law of Christ takes the Pentateuch (including the ten commandments) and sums it up as: '"You shall love the Lord your God with all your heart and with all your soul and with all your mind." This is the greatest and first commandment. And a second is like it: "You shall love your neighbour as yourself." On these two commandments hang all the Law and the Prophets' (Matthew 22:37–40).

In Christ a little can go a long way, and quality is better than quantity. In fact the crowd do not even need two fish (there are twelve baskets of leftovers – enough for each disciple or tribe of Israel): one is enough. For Jesus is the one fish – the *ichthus* in Greek – which was to become and remains a symbol of Christianity, and it is in Christ alone that all our needs are met.

You, Christ, are all we need, feed us always with your law and your love. Amen.

GORDON GILES

Friday 13 June   **John 2:6–10 (NRSV, abridged)**

Six water jars

Now standing there were six stone water jars for the Jewish rites of purification, each holding twenty or thirty gallons. Jesus said to them, 'Fill the jars with water.' And they filled them up to the brim. He said to them, 'Now draw some out, and take it to the person in charge of the banquet.' So they took it. When the person in charge tasted the water that had become wine and did not know where it came from… that person… said… 'Everyone serves the good wine first and then the inferior wine after the guests have become drunk. But you have kept the good wine until now.'

In Galilee there is a church dedicated to the marriage at Cana. Couples get married or renew their vows there. Wine is sold: sweet for Holy Communion or good-quality Israeli table wine. There can be something special about using a bottle of wine bought in Cana for Holy Communion. The wine is not as it was in Jesus' day, but that it comes from Galilee adds a spiritual special effect, so to speak.

The wedding at Cana is about wine, marriage and change. It is Jesus' first miracle, a sign of things to come. Generally the water, and the jars which contain it, are overlooked. In the modern Cana church, there is one in the lower area, and it is very large. These jars – of which we are told there were six – hold about 25 gallons (about 114 litres or twice the petrol tank of an average car). The water was used for washing feet and other rituals. But why six jars?

Some people say that six is the number of humanity – a number which falls short of perfection, symbolised by the number seven. Similarly in Revelation we find the infamous 666 – three sixes – a perfect number (3) of imperfection (6). Threefold imperfection comes close, deceptively so even. So it may be that Jesus turning six large jars of foot water into wine tells us something about God doing something miraculous with imperfect humanity.

Alongside symbolism in the story there is also plain matter-of-fact, eye-witness detail: there were six water jars, not five, nor seven, but simply six.

Jesus, turn the matter-of-fact water of our lives into the greatest vintage in the kingdom of heaven. Amen.

GORDON GILES

Saturday 14 June   **Genesis 29:18, 20, 26–27, 30b (NRSV)**

Seven years for seven days

Jacob loved Rachel, so he said, 'I will serve you seven years for your younger daughter Rachel'… So Jacob served seven years for Rachel, and they seemed to him but a few days because of his love for her… Laban said, 'This is not done in our country – giving the younger before the firstborn. Complete the week of this one, and we will give you the other also in return for serving me another seven years'… [Jacob] loved Rachel more than Leah. He served Laban for another seven years.

There are several sevens in this story, literally so. Jacob does a deal with Laban, the father of Leah and Rachel, for the hand of Rachel in marriage, but at the wedding Leah is substituted and Jacob ends up in bed with her instead. He renegotiates another seven years' work for a second bride. This all happens before the codification of a law in Leviticus 18:18, which says: 'You shall not take a woman as a rival to her sister, uncovering her nakedness while her sister is still alive.' We need not infer anything symbolic in the seven years he worked: that was simply the price, which seemed 'but a few days'. The 'week' is the seven-day honeymoon.

Jacob was a deceiver, who conned his brother Esau out of his birthright, and now it is his turn to be stitched up. Meanwhile Leah, whose marriage prospects appear to have not been as promising as her sister's, secures a husband and becomes the mother of five of the tribes of Israel: Reuben, Simeon, Levi, Judah, and later Issachar and Zebulun, and a daughter Dinah. Jacob also has children by Rachel's maid Bilhah (Dan and Naphtali) and Leah's maid Zilpah (Gad and Asher). Finally, Jacob has two sons with Rachel: Joseph and Benjamin. The fact that the boys give their names to the tribes of Israel and Dinah does not, and that Jacob has relations with four women who are all effectively of the same household reflects sexual politics and practices which surprise and even annoy us today. Nevertheless, God acted through it all, raising up the great tribes of Israel from a dysfunctional and damaged family.

O Lord, work good through the muddles and failings of our lives to the honour of your holy name. Amen.

GORDON GILES

Sunday 15 June   Luke 2:19–21 (NRSV)

Eighth day

Mary treasured all these words and pondered them in her heart. The shepherds returned, glorifying and praising God for all they had heard and seen, just as it had been told them. When the eighth day came, it was time to circumcise the child, and he was called Jesus, the name given by the angel before he was conceived in the womb.

Sunday is known as the eighth day of creation, which is why baptismal fonts are often octagonal. Creation took six days, then a day of rest – the sabbath (Genesis 2:1–2) – and then, with the resurrection of Jesus comes a new start – like a new week (John 20:1). This became known as the Lord's Day (Sunday), as it succeeds the sabbath (Saturday) and reminds us that in Jesus a new 'week of creation' commences: a new testament to the saving love of God.

Meanwhile the historic and spiritual aspects of circumcision on the eighth day mean that the newborn baby has experienced at least one sabbath before the event. Circumcision is the sign of covenant given to Abraham (Genesis 17:9–14), administered on the eighth day. Ritually speaking it means that the mother is free to attend and nurse the baby boy immediately afterwards; any earlier might prove difficult in terms of mobility, health and hygiene. Medically speaking, the child needs not only to have survived, but to have gained some strength for the procedure. It has become apparent in recent years that eight days is the optimum for enough vitamin K to have built up in the child's body, which aids the clotting of blood. As is so often the case, with Jewish food laws, for example, the ancient Jewish practice enshrined in law and tradition contains what we would now call scientific wisdom which was understood but not articulated at the time.

Jesus was circumcised on the eighth day because that was the Jewish law and the tradition, but it was also a good idea: if one is going to do this sort of thing, the eighth day is best. That it also prefigures the day of resurrection a lifetime later is a profound and serendipitous symbolic twist.

God and Father of all creation, renew your covenant with all your children, that on the last day we may see you face to face. Amen.

GORDON GILES

Monday 16 June   **Mark 15:22, 24–25, 33 (NRSV)**

Nine o'clock

Then they brought Jesus to the place called Golgotha (which means the Place of a Skull)… And they crucified him and divided his clothes among them, casting lots to decide what each should take. It was nine o'clock in the morning when they crucified him… When it was noon, darkness came over the whole land until three in the afternoon.

Many churches observe a Good Friday tradition of three hours at the cross, usually between noon and 3.00 pm. Yet Mark says Jesus was crucified at 9.00 am.

In ancient Jewish tradition, noon was the sixth hour of the day and the first hour was at dawn. The King James (Authorized) Version of this passage says Jesus was crucified at the third hour. Darkness covers the land from the sixth to the ninth hours. So Jesus spent six hours on the cross, not three. John's account of the crucifixion is not as detailed as the other gospel writers, and he does not say at what time Jesus died, while the others tell us it was at the ninth hour – 3.00 pm. Some commentators therefore conclude that Pilate sentenced Jesus earlier in the day (perhaps as early as 6.00 am), that Jesus was nailed to the cross at 9.00 am, at noon darkness covered the land, and at 3.00 pm it was all finished and Jesus 'gave up the ghost' (John 19:30, KJV).

Noon is the sixth hour because it is midway through the twelve-hour light part of day; the night was also deemed to be twelve hours long, throughout the year. The evening therefore began at 6.00 pm and that is why there was a need to ensure the bodies were buried before the end of the day at 6.00 pm (see John 19:31–34).

Nowadays we are governed by clock time, and we think of night as taking up a third, not half of the day: the time when we are asleep. God's time is different: it is eternal. As God's time intersects with human existence, like the vertical and horizontal beams of a cross, we are reminded that all our clock-watching is but a shadow of the greater reality in which God the Father sends his Son into the world that none may perish, but have eternal life.

Father God, we thank you for sending us your Son to fill our time with the eternal promise of resurrection life. Amen.

GORDON GILES

Tuesday 17 June   **Psalm 33:1–3 (NRSV)**

Ten strings

Rejoice in the Lord, O you righteous. Praise befits the upright. Praise the Lord with the lyre; make melody to him with the harp of ten strings. Sing to him a new song; play skilfully on the strings, with loud shouts.

The ten-stringed harp is known as an asor and was about three feet tall; its strings were divided into two sets of five. A modern scale has eight notes. The ancient Greeks had eight different, named, scales – known as modes– each of which involved different sets of intervals between the notes, creating a distinctive sound for each mode. Different modes were deployed for particular situations. They ultimately formed the basis of plainsong and then our western scales.

Meanwhile in the east there were five-note (pentatonic) scales. To get a sense of the sound of pentatonic music, simply play the piano using only the black keys. Doing so, however randomly, can sound exotic to western ears. The fact that the Jewish harp was divided into two sets of five strings might tempt us to suppose that the strings were tuned to two pentatonic scales. It is possible, but unlikely.

More significantly the division of the ten strings into two fives mirrors the two tablets of Moses' law – the ten commandments. The instrument – and therefore the sound it made – symbolised and embodied the pattern of God's law. In this it was not so unlike the idea the Greeks had, who believed their music echoed the music of the spheres – the universe.

Our modern music sounds very different because we use one pattern of intervals between notes, for all scales. Differences in intonation between different pitched scales have been ironed out since the 17th century, which means the 'temperament' of each scale is now equal. This was not so for David's (Jewish) harp: the music of the psalmist's days sounded very different to ours.

Yet we still sing of the law and the love of the Lord. Like our modern faith, it has changed tonality, yet it is the same. This is the paradoxical power of faith: same ten commandments, same Father, same Son, same Holy Spirit – who inspires the music of our praise in every age.

God, may we praise you with all our heartstrings. Amen.

GORDON GILES

Wednesday 18 June — Mark 16:14–16 (NRSV)

Eleven men

> Later he appeared to the eleven themselves as they were sitting at the table, and he upbraided them for their lack of faith and stubbornness, because they had not believed those who saw him after he had risen. And he said to them, 'Go into all the world and proclaim the good news to the whole creation. The one who believes and is baptised will be saved, but the one who does not believe will be condemned.'

This is not a comfortable account of a post-resurrection appearance of Jesus to the remaining eleven disciples. Like a pep talk to a team who have just lost the match, missed opportunities to score and failed to tackle the opposition, Jesus the team captain 'upbraids' them for their inadequacies. Other post-resurrection stories are lighter in tone, but we recall that in the upper room Thomas receives a robust response when he has said he will not believe without evidence (John 20:24–29), and on the beach at breakfast, Jesus gives Peter a talking-to (John 21:15–19). Matthew's gospel has little, save the instruction to go and baptise. In Luke the focus is on his teaching the eleven how to interpret the scriptures and the predictions he made.

Sometimes we may want to think of the 'cuddly' Jesus – the good shepherd who loves, searches for and saves us, but there is a harder edge to his teaching, ministry, death and resurrection. The final chapter of Mark's gospel resonates with some of these other encounters after the resurrection, but historically some have questioned its authenticity. Nevertheless it is in our Bibles for our instruction and learning. It shows us another aspect of those remarkable days after the resurrection, when emotions were raw, tensions high and credibility challenged. Jesus is stern, yet still loving, for the benefit of Team Apostles and the greater goal of salvation towards which he was determined to point them and in which cause had spent three years training them.

As we read the Bible, we hear Jesus' voice in many tones and contexts. All remind us of our call to missionary love and eternal truth, revealed through Christ's suffering and promised in his resurrection.

Jesus, help us to hear your call to mission and remind us always of your loving mercy. Amen.

GORDON GILES

Thursday 19 June   **Matthew 29:27–28 (NRSV)**

Twelve disciples

Then Peter said in reply, 'Look, we have left everything and followed you. What then will we have?' Jesus said to them, 'Truly I tell you, at the renewal of all things, when the Son of Man is seated on the throne of his glory, you who have followed me will also sit on twelve thrones, judging the twelve tribes of Israel.'

There are dozens of twelves in the Bible. They mostly relate to the twelve tribes of Israel, directly or symbolically (see Genesis 49:28). Jacob has twelve sons, each 'founds' a tribe, and they pervade the Bible all the way to Revelation, where multiplied, they become the 144,000 (12,000 from each tribe). Similarly, in Revelation we find twelve gates and twelve foundations of the New Jerusalem (Revelation 21—22).

That there were twelve tribes of Israel and also twelve named disciples is so obvious it is so often overlooked, forgotten or ignored. As we shall see tomorrow, when Judas dies he is replaced to make up the twelve. The connection with authority and governance is strong, and the apostles represent the twelve tribes in an expansive, salvation-for-all sense. They are not Jewish priests or hereditary peers; rather they are those who have been chosen to spread the gospel far and wide. They will speak and teach from personal experience.

Interestingly, there is not much insistence in Christian churches for leadership to fall in dozens – the early churches did not stipulate this and formed their own governance structures, based on the disciples' work and ministry, but not on their number. An exception perhaps is the medieval College of Minor Canons of St Paul's Cathedral, which was made up of 'up to twelve' clergy. The college, of which I was once a member, was abolished in 2016.

While there were twelve male apostles, echoing the culture and heritage of the twelve tribes of Israel, there were other disciples, and there is no evidence to suggest that Jesus had no female followers, nor that they exercised no leadership or authority in the early church. The twelve apostles are those who carry the faith back to the past and forward to the future, to our own day and beyond.

Lord Jesus, here I am. Call me. Amen.

GORDON GILES

Friday 20 June   **Acts 1:22b–26a (NRSV)**

Thirteenth man

'One of these must become a witness with us to his resurrection.' So they proposed two, Joseph called Barsabbas, who was also known as Justus, and Matthias. Then they prayed and said, 'Lord, you know everyone's heart. Show us which one of these two you have chosen to take the place in this ministry and apostleship from which Judas turned aside to go to his own place.' And they cast lots for them, and the lot fell on Matthias.

Gambling is about numbers. Lotteries and raffles are founded on the random selection of (sets of) numbers, and probability applies: if there are ten balls in the bag you have a ten per cent chance of winning. As the permutations increase the chances of winning becomes significantly reduced. Nevertheless, someone must win (we assume) and so even with very low odds tickets are bought. Yet it is all luck – mostly tough luck – and most people do not – if ever – win. Even where it is a simple case of heads or tails, or the short straw, as in the selection of Judas' replacement, someone (in this case, Justus) does not win.

Did God favour Matthias? Or is it that God would have been content with whoever they chose, even if they did use a pagan lottery method to make the decision? Nowadays application forms, psychometric tests, interviews and references would be sought to narrow down candidates for a church leadership role. Vocation is important and in those days, just as today, it blended with contemporary secular methodology to attempt to ensure that the person with the best fit 'gets the job'.

Matthias, the winner, becomes 13th apostle, and Justus (Joseph Barsabbas) loses out. We never hear of him again (unless he is the 'Judas Barsabbas' of Acts 15:22). Yet he is still a disciple, even if not numbered among the first team of saints, and he is still a missionary of Christ loved by God, like millions after him. In one sense he is the disciple to whom we can most easily relate. He is the one who works behind the scenes, gets overlooked, misses out on fame, works hard for the kingdom and thus represents so many unnamed, yet numbered saints.

Lord Jesus, may we be content with our calling and never seek status or recognition other than that of being yours. Amen.

GORDON GILES

Saturday 21 June   Matthew 1:16–17 (NRSV)

Fourteen generations

Jacob the father of Joseph the husband of Mary, who bore Jesus, who is called the Messiah. So all the generations from Abraham to David are fourteen generations; and from David to the deportation to Babylon, fourteen generations; and from the deportation to Babylon to the Messiah, fourteen generations.

Matthew's genealogy is a rollcall of honour. That Jesus is directly descended from Abraham is very important to the Jews whom Matthew was evangelising and trying to unite with a timeline of universal salvation hinged on David.

Matthew seemed to like numbers, but was not that good at them (he was a tax collector!) There are actually only 13 generations in the first and third sets in Matthew 1:1–17, and 14 in the middle set of names, making a total of 40 generations, which might correspond to the 40 years of wilderness wandering or days of Christ's temptation. However, the key to the list is David (*Dawid*), the letters of whose palindromic name add up to 14: D-4, W-6, D-4 (no vowels exist in Hebrew). For numerical-theological reasons, 42 generations are claimed, and Matthew implies it was not really very long between Abraham and David and Christ.

King David was very real to Jesus' generation, and Matthew carries his readers to and from the time before Christ. Reading it now, we note that we need only go back 33 sixty-year lifetimes to meet Christ: the events of the Bible are more recent than we might imagine. We gain not only a sense of Jesus' place in history, but of the pace of history.

It is not only *who* you know, but *what* you know. In Matthew's catalogue of spiritual greatness lie strands of wisdom, passed from father to son, and in Ruth's case through a daughter. Religious leaders revere those at whose feet they sat, learning from widely respected elders, passing on received wisdom. Here Jesus, at birth, is presented as following in the sacred footsteps of a wide range of reverends. Alongside his heavenly Father and his earthly father Joseph, he also had three Davids-worth of generations of spiritual fathers.

God, help us never to forget the heritage of faith,
truth and wisdom in which we stand. Amen.

GORDON GILES

Introduction

Esther

I first heard Esther's story as a child in nightly instalments, told by my grandfather, who was a master storyteller. Now I cannot fathom how he succeeded in making such a dark story accessible to children, but such was his gift. Here we have a narrative that tells of slavery, oppression, harems and indulgent leadership. There is an evil villain, Haman, who plots mass genocide, while the protagonists, Esther and Mordecai, act with wisdom, integrity, courage and self-sacrifice. We read of wrongs being righted, justice being done, the salvation of God's people, celebration and longed-for security. In spite of the darkness, at each step of the narrative God appears to be working his purposes out with ever-increasing involvement, although of course he is always active, even at the times when he seems hidden or does not get named.

We do not know who wrote the book of Esther, although possible authors have been proposed, one being the hero himself, Mordecai. Without mentioning God, his covenant with his people or prayer, the author wants to demonstrate that there is a God in heaven who has ultimate control, working actively in the lives of his people. At the same time the writer shows the importance of human responsibility in shaping events. This is the mystery of the interaction between God's sovereignty and human will. God choses to work through those who are committed to his purposes.

The book of Esther is important to us because it is part of *our* story. God's plan for humanity depended on the survival of the Judahites, for the Messiah was to come from the line of Judah. God promised Abraham (Judah's great-grandfather) that all people, us included, will be blessed through him. By faith in Jesus Christ, we, the church, have been 'grafted' on to 'Abraham's tree' (Romans 11).

Over the next fortnight we delve into a book that challenges us to godly transformation in response to our circumstances, to a renewal in our thinking and to a willingness to take action. We are encouraged to trust God who, even when he appears absent, is working all things together for good.

May we confidently say with Job, 'I know that you can do all things and that no purpose of yours can be thwarted' (Job 42:2, NRSV).

FIONA STRATTA

Sunday 22 June   **Esther 1:10–12 (NLT, abridged)**

Vashti's protest

On the seventh day of the feast, when King Xerxes was in high spirits because of the wine, he told the seven eunuchs who attended him… to bring Queen Vashti to him with the royal crown on her head. He wanted the nobles and all the other men to gaze on her beauty, for she was a very beautiful woman. But when they conveyed the king's order to Queen Vashti, she refused to come. This made the king furious, and he burned with anger.

It is 483BC and Xerxes, ruler of the Persian empire, is giving a final banquet for his nobles, officials and military leaders after six months of planning a war against Greece. His bubble of pride and joviality is burst when Queen Vashti refuses to be paraded in front of his guests. How is he to react? If he cannot control outcomes within the palace, how can he control outcomes across his empire? We can only imagine Vashti's reasons for this seemingly small act of defiance, but it is seen by the king's advisors as a threat to the stability of their patriarchal society. Vashti pays the high price of banishment.

Many since have acted in defiance of an order untenable to them. For some, this has led to a loss of a position and status (as for Vashti); for others it has culminated in martyrdom. However, in some cases the small protest has been the beginning of a major change in the course of history. The civil rights movement in the USA was initiated by Rosa Park's refusal to give up her seat on a bus to a white man. Worldwide, both the abolition of slavery and the suffrage movements grew from small beginnings as individuals courageously and tenaciously fought for equality.

As followers of Christ, we need to be prepared for opportunities for godly protest that come our way, when we can show in word or action that 'there is no longer Jew or Gentile, slave or free, male and female. For you are all one in Christ Jesus' (Galatians 3:28).

Thank you, Lord, that you have told us what it is that you require from us: to act justly, love mercy and walk humbly with you (Micah 6:8). Amen.

FIONA STRATTA

Monday 23 June   **Esther 2:5–7 (NLT, abridged)**

Mordecai's commitment

At that time there was a Jewish man in the fortress of Susa whose name was Mordecai son of Jair. He was from the tribe of Benjamin… His family had been among those who, with King Jehoiachin of Judah, had been exiled from Jerusalem to Babylon by King Nebuchadnezzar. This man had a very beautiful and lovely young cousin, Hadassah, who was also called Esther. When her father and mother died, Mordecai adopted her into his family and raised her as his own daughter.

Mordecai's family were exiled a hundred years previously, and about 50 years later Zerubbabel took the first group of exiles back to Jerusalem. Yet some Judahites have chosen to stay within the security of Persia, where under Cyrus the Great (the first Persian emperor) they have been allowed to start businesses, take positions in the government and practise their faith. Mordecai works in an administrative role in Xerxes' winter palace in Susa. We learn immediately that he is a man of integrity, faithfulness and compassion, capable of the self-sacrifice needed to bring up his relatives' orphaned child. Mordecai goes far beyond the call of duty by raising her lovingly as a daughter.

During World War II, homes across Britain welcomed Jewish refugees and children evacuated from the cities. For some, this initial compulsion to help grew into a Mordecai-like loving commitment. Those who cared for my father-in-law as an evacuee child would have willingly adopted him at the end of the war. However, in the years they devotedly looked after him while living out their Christian faith, they passed on to him a lasting legacy as they planted seeds of trust in Jesus Christ. They gave him an example of what it is to have confidence in God, just as Mordecai did for Esther so long ago.

We may not have the inner or outer resources, or the opportunity, to open our homes in big gestures of compassion. However, as we walk with Jesus, small gestures of compassion can encourage others and perhaps be life-changing for them. The ripple effect may be beyond our imagining.

Lord, through your power at work within us, may you accomplish infinitely more than we might ask or think (Ephesians 3:20). Amen.

FIONA STRATTA

Tuesday 24 June   **Esther 2:8–9, 15b (NLT)**

Hegai's favourite

As a result of the king's decree, Esther, along with many other young women, was brought to the king's harem at the fortress of Susa and placed in Hegai's care. Hegai was very impressed with Esther and treated her kindly. He quickly ordered a special menu for her and provided her with beauty treatments. He also assigned her seven maids specially chosen for the king's palace, and he moved her and her maids into the best place in the harem… When it was Esther's turn to go to the king, she accepted the advice of Hegai, the eunuch in charge of the harem. She asked for nothing except what he suggested, and she was admired by everyone who saw her.

Esther is likely to have been a teenager when she is forced to leave the loving security she has known to enter the harem. Her vulnerability is abused when she is forcefully recruited for sexual exploitation, an evil that tragically continues to this day. Her terror and trauma must have been immense. Yet she behaves in such a way that it is more than her beauty which impresses Hegai, gaining his favour. In spite of being powerless to escape her situation, we get a sense of Esther's poise and courage as she listens, learns and takes Hegai's advice in the year before she is sent to the king.

External events are outside of Esther's influence, as are the thoughts, feelings, beliefs and behaviour of others. Yet, even in difficult circumstances, she takes responsibility for the one thing she can control: her reaction, both to her situation and to the people around her. Like Esther, by identifying what we can and cannot influence, we are then in a position to work on our attitudes and behaviour. We have the presence of the Holy Spirit as we do this, drawing alongside us to guide and counsel.

Although the enslaved Esther finds favour (and the eventual climax of the narrative is freedom for God's people), the abuse of human rights should never be condoned. Through prayer, support and action we need to fight against injustice and abuse in all its forms, whether close to home or far away.

Thank you, Lord, that your hand sustains and your arm strengthens us (Psalm 89:21). Amen.

FIONA STRATTA

Wednesday 25 June   **Esther 2:10–11, 19–20 (NLT)**

Wisdom and hope

Esther had not told anyone of her nationality and family background, because Mordecai had directed her not to do so. Every day Mordecai would take a walk near the courtyard of the harem to find out about Esther and what was happening to her… Even after all the young women had been transferred to the second harem and Mordecai had become a palace official, Esther continued to keep her family background and nationality a secret. She was still following Mordecai's directions, just as she did when she lived in his home.

Mordecai shows his commitment to supporting Esther by daily enquiries after her well-being. His counsel that she should keep her nationality a secret indicates that, despite the relative religious freedom the Judahites are granted in Persia, there is enough of a threat to warrant silence. When Esther becomes the king's favourite and replaces Vashti as queen, Mordecai's warning keeps her grounded and she continues to respect his astuteness. Esther's humility leads to a wisdom that is to benefit not only her, but all God's people.

At this point in the story, Mordecai uses his position as Esther's mentor and father figure to advise and protect her. We can imagine his sorrow as he follows Esther's progress through that first year and then her placement in the second harem, where Esther is sent after her night with the king. Mentoring and parenting are costly privileges, ones that drive us to a deeper dependence on the Lord, the source of wisdom and hope.

The writer of Ecclesiastes tells us that there is 'a time to be silent and a time to speak' (3:7), as the story of Esther shows so clearly. For Esther, surrounded by other young women, the pull to tell her story must have been strong. However, she shows restraint, being quick to listen, yet slow to speak. In practice, it can be challenging for us to know when to be silent and when to speak, yet God promises us generous amounts of wisdom when we ask for it.

Lord, thank you for your promise of wisdom which, like honey, is of great benefit to us. May we be wise, hope-filled people, whose carefully chosen words are sweet and healing (Proverbs 16:24; 24:14). Amen.

FIONA STRATTA

Thursday 26 June   **Esther 2:21–22, 23b (NLT)**

The right place at the right time

One day as Mordecai was on duty at the king's gate, two of the king's eunuchs, Bigthana and Teresh – who were guards at the door of the king's private quarters – became angry at King Xerxes and plotted to assassinate him. But Mordecai heard about the plot and gave the information to Queen Esther. She then told the king about it and gave Mordecai credit for the report… This was all recorded in *The Book of the History of King Xerxes' Reign*.

As the story develops we have an increasing awareness of God being at work 'behind the scenes'. This has already been hinted at, such as in the way Esther won Hegai's favour, leading to blessings in her dark situation. Mordecai, the right person, happens to be in exactly the right place at the right time to save the king's life. He is the right person for the task because he will act wisely and with integrity. Although credit is given to Mordecai in the narrative, there is no immediate reward.

Like Mordecai, much of our daily lives may seem to go by with a quiet mindfulness of God's presence. There are, however, moments when we know that we have been at exactly the right place at the right time. What seemed like a coincidence is actually a 'God-incidence'. Journalling such moments can encourage us in our faith journey. It is all too easy to forget.

Mordecai is God's person for the job, not only because he can be trusted to take action, but also because he can be entrusted with being overlooked. At this point there is no accolade; work continues as usual. No doubt we share the experience of having been overlooked, whether in secular work, Christian service or in the giving of sacrificial love which has not been recognised or affirmed. First, we can take comfort from the fact that God sees and delights in us. Second, we can choose to reject bitterness and ask the Holy Spirit to use the experience to transform us into the likeness of Jesus Christ.

Lord, change us as we fix our eyes on you, the author and perfector of our faith (Hebrews 12:2). May we be ready for God-incidences and prepared to be overlooked. Amen.

FIONA STRATTA

Friday 27 June   **Esther 3:1–2, 5–6 (NLT, abridged)**

Haman's anger

Some time later King Xerxes promoted Haman son of Hammedatha the Agagite over all the other nobles, making him the most powerful official in the empire. All the king's officials would bow down before Haman to show him respect whenever he passed by, for so the king had commanded. But Mordecai refused to bow down or show him respect... Haman... was filled with rage. He had learned of Mordecai's nationality, so he decided it was not enough to lay hands on Mordecai alone. Instead, he looked for a way to destroy all the Jews throughout the entire empire of Xerxes.

Xerxes makes an unwise choice in promoting Haman to be his right-hand man, for Haman, like the king, has a problem with anger management. Haman is enraged when Mordecai will not bow down to him. It provides him with an excuse to vent his hatred: he plans ethnic cleansing throughout the empire, the killing of all Judahites. In his sermon on the mount, Jesus teaches that wrong actions start with wrong heart attitudes, such as anger leading to hatred and murder. It is for good reason that we are warned in the Bible not to let the sun go down on our anger (Ephesians 4:26).

Why did Mordecai refuse to bow down to Haman? The narrative gives no explanation for Mordecai's refusal. Bowing down to someone in a superior position does not necessarily have to infer that Haman is being acknowledged as a deity, although perhaps Mordecai saw it as this and therefore refused. Their ancestry may also have played a part in Mordecai's decision, for Haman was a descendant of Agag, who was an Amalekite king. God's people and the Amalekites were always enemies. Mordecai did what he considered right and God-honouring at that moment in time.

Taking a stand for what we believe is right, whether through passive resistance or through action, is never a guarantee that all will go well from a human perspective. We are often unaware of the possible consequences. It is then we learn to trust in God's grace and sovereignty, believing that 'all manner of thing shall be well' (Julian of Norwich).

Lord, thank you that your goodness and mercy follows us all the days of our lives (Psalm 23:6). Amen.

FIONA STRATTA

Saturday 28 June   **Esther 3:7, 11; 4:1 (NLT, abridged)**

Lament

So in the month of April… lots were cast in Haman's presence (the lots were called purim*) to determine the best day and month to take action. And the day selected was March 7, nearly a year later… The king said, 'The money and the people are both yours to do with as you see fit'… When Mordecai learned about all that had been done, he tore his clothes, put on burlap and ashes, and went out into the city, crying with a loud and bitter wail.*

How terrible it must have been for Mordecai to learn of Haman's plans to annihilate the Judahites. Did he feel responsible? Although it is true that Mordecai's passive resistance preceded the ensuing events, Haman makes his wicked plan from a stance of hatred for God's people. He is responsible before God for his actions. The Lord sees what he does and examines the path he takes. Haman will bring about his own downfall; no one else is to blame. It is easy to lose sight of personal responsibility and to blame others or circumstances for our choices or behaviour.

Mordecai makes known his bitter grief. His desperation for his people is as public as his refusal to bow to Haman. The wearing of burlap (a coarse material) is a symbol of grief, remorse and repentance. The discomfort of the cloth is an outer sign of the discomfort of the soul. But such behaviour is not court etiquette, drawing further attention to Mordecai.

Are we afraid to show grief? On our screens, we see outpourings of lament in war-torn parts of the world where it is normal to display grief openly. We have much to learn from this in our more reserved societies, for how can we address what has never been expressed? Jesus, moved by compassion, shed tears publicly. The psalms can help us, for they are full of laments that enable us to shape our grief into words and prayers. They also give us a resource to weep with those who weep.

Lord, thank you that we can pour out our hearts to you, for you are our refuge (Psalm 62:8). God of comfort, may we know your comfort in sorrow and share this comfort with others (2 Corinthians 1:3–4). Amen.

FIONA STRATTA

Sunday 29 June   **Esther 4:13–14 (NLT)**

For such a time as this

Mordecai sent this reply to Esther: 'Don't think for a moment that because you're in the palace you will escape when all other Jews are killed. If you keep quiet at a time like this, deliverance and relief for the Jews will arise from some other place, but you and your relatives will die. Who knows if perhaps you were made queen for just such a time as this?'

'For such a time as this' is undoubtedly the most well-known phrase from the book of Esther. Esther has refused Mordecai's first request that she should approach the king to tell him about the plight of her people. However, Mordecai does not take no for an answer, believing in God's sovereignty and the possibility that Esther's position of influence may well be part of God's plan for the deliverance of the Judahites.

He does not say, 'You were definitely made queen for just such a time as this,' but rather: 'Perhaps you were made queen...' Here we see Mordecai's wisdom and humility at work once again – humility in that he does not claim to know God's plan and purposes; wisdom in that his knowledge and understanding of the scriptures give him evidence that God chooses and uses courageous, obedient and self-sacrificing individuals to further his story. We need this humility and wisdom when planning and hoping for the future, saying in our hearts *Deo volente*, 'God willing'. It is wise to be cautious when others categorically claim to know exactly how God has told them he will act or in making any such claims ourselves.

However, it is conceivable to Mordecai that the Lord God is making a way that only Esther can tread. Nevertheless, should she choose not to walk this path, God will deliver his people in another way. This is a tremendous reassurance to us: we need not anxiously carry burdens of responsibility, feeling that it is all down to us. God alone bears the 'weight of the world on his shoulders'.

Lord God, thank you for creating us in Christ Jesus to do good works (Ephesians 2:10. We acknowledge that it is you who works in us to will and fulfil your purposes (Philippians 2:13). Amen.

FIONA STRATTA

Monday 30 June   **Esther 4:15–17 (NLT)**

Not my will, but yours

Then Esther sent this reply to Mordecai: 'Go and gather together all the Jews of Susa and fast for me. Do not eat or drink for three days, night or day. My maids and I will do the same. And then, though it is against the law, I will go in to see the king. If I must die, I must die.' So Mordecai went away and did everything as Esther had ordered him.

In the Bible prayer and fasting go together, so we can assume that prayer accompanied the three days and nights of fasting. Esther calls on *all* God's people to fast at the same time. Many of the biblical reasons for prayer and fasting seem to be present in this communal fast: an urgent crying out for deliverance; a plea for victory in a spiritual and earthly battle; a demonstration of profound grief; a humbling and preparation of Esther for her ministry and the seeking of God's wisdom, guidance and empowerment to fulfil her calling.

Esther has learnt, in all likelihood from Mordecai, that there is power to be found in prayer and fasting, and that her courage will be strengthened in knowing that others are joining her in spiritual warfare. Jesus' teaching on both prayer and fasting assumes these practices to be part of the disciple's rhythm of life. Prayer and fasting open the way to humbling ourselves before God. It is not a way to pressurise God to do our will, but rather a discipline that helps us to draw near to him so that his sovereign will becomes clearer to us.

When Esther declares, 'If I must die, I must die', we recognise her submission to God's call, perhaps after a long internal struggle. We sense that she has courage but knows fear, she has faith but knows doubt. So we do not despair when we find fear and doubt in our hearts, knowing that they may run in parallel with courage and faith. Together they teach us to move forwards in humility, depending on God and acknowledging our need for spiritual support from others.

Father God, we believe, help our unbelief (Mark 9:24).
Strengthen us to pray, as Jesus prayed in Gethsemane,
'Not my will, but yours' (Luke 22:42). Amen.

FIONA STRATTA

Tuesday 1 July — **Esther 5:1–4 (NLT, abridged)**

One step at a time

On the third day of the fast, Esther put on her royal robes and entered the inner court of the palace... The king was sitting on his royal throne, facing the entrance. When he saw Queen Esther standing there... he welcomed her and held out the gold sceptre to her. So Esther approached and touched the end of the sceptre. Then the king asked her, 'What do you want, Queen Esther?'... And Esther replied, 'If it please the king, let the king and Haman come today to a banquet I have prepared for the king.'

Today's reading describes the moment when Esther's inner transformation shows itself in a brave act. She is starting on a journey towards declaring her solidarity with the people of God in the hope of saving them. Esther does not rush in immediately with her request. So why could this be?

First, the invitation to dinner was typical of middle-eastern graciousness and politeness before making a request. Second, in accepting the invitation and receiving hospitality, the king was deepening his relationship with Esther and increasing his commitment to honouring her wishes. Third, it is a month since the king asked for her; potentially she may have lost his favour. In a society with no securities, she must go cautiously. A dinner invitation for the king and his chief official is a safe start. Wisdom has been prayed for, and wisdom has been given.

We do not know from reading the narrative whether God had revealed the whole plan to Esther or whether he revealed one step at a time. She may well not have realised until far into the first banquet that the time was not yet right: the king was still not genuinely ready, in spite of his promises, to fight for her cause. A second banquet would be necessary.

The Almighty, all-seeing God often only shows us one step at a time on our life journey. We walk by lamplight, not by floodlight. Lamplight teaches us to trust in the dark, to take one step believing that the next one will become clear. It is God's wise way of inviting us to travel with him.

Lord, give us the wisdom and patience not to rush into situations. May we rest in your timing. Amen.

FIONA STRATTA

Wednesday 2 July Esther 6:1–6 (NLT, abridged)

The tables turn

That night the king had trouble sleeping, so he ordered an attendant to bring the book of the history of his reign… In those records he discovered an account of how Mordecai had exposed the plot… to assassinate King Xerxes. 'What reward or recognition did we ever give Mordecai for this?' the king asked. His attendants replied, 'Nothing has been done for him'… As it happened, Haman had just arrived… to ask the king to impale Mordecai on the pole he had prepared… The king said, 'What should I do to honour a man who truly pleases me?'

Here we see God at work in the details – even a sleepless night can be divinely ordained! The king uses his night hours to listen to his annals and, as a result, at last Mordecai is to be rewarded for his service to the king. This happens at exactly the right moment; a day later and it would have been too late for Mordecai. This biblical experience of God coming through at the last minute may well be one that resonates with us.

The battle is raging between good and evil, for while the king's favour for Mordecai is growing, Haman is planning to have Mordecai killed. Paul reminds us that in seemingly human and material situations, we can in reality be struggling against the spiritual forces of evil in the heavenly realms (Ephesians 6:12).

Xerxes turns to Haman for advice on how best to reward a man who has served the king well. This is a dark narrative, and yet there is humour to be found in the dramatic irony: Haman has no sooner planned Mordecai's demise when he unwittingly plans Mordecai's advancement, while all the time assuming that he is the one to be honoured.

Pride comes before a fall: Haman has the humiliation of leading a splendidly attired Mordecai around the city on the king's own horse. By contrast, Mordecai has learnt to walk humbly with God through trial and tribulation; he neither breaks nor brags.

Lord, may we be prepared for our struggles by wearing the belt of truth, the breastplate of righteousness, the shoes of peace, the shield of faith, the helmet of salvation and the sword of the Spirit (Ephesians 6:13–17). Amen.

FIONA STRATTA

Thursday 3 July   **Esther 7:1–6 (NLT, abridged)**

The second banquet

So the king and Haman went to Queen Esther's banquet… the king again said to Esther, 'Tell me what you want, Queen Esther'… Queen Esther replied, 'If I have found favour with the king, and if it pleases the king to grant my request, I ask that my life and the lives of my people will be spared. For my people and I have been sold to those who would kill, slaughter, and annihilate us…' 'Who would do such a thing?' King Xerxes demanded… Esther replied, 'This wicked Haman is our adversary and our enemy.'

During the second banquet prepared for Xerxes and Haman, Esther knows that the time to speak out has come. She moves centre stage while in the wings stands the pole erected by Haman. Persuasively Esther fights for the cause of her people using powerful language: kill, slaughter, annihilate. Carefully she avoids assertiveness, the cause of Vashti's downfall. Then the moment comes, and she speaks with power and authority.

Esther illustrates the truth of the words 'If God is for us, who can ever be against us?' (Romans 8:31). A humble girl rises to be queen and defeats the second most powerful man in Persia. Haman, who has no value for innocent lives, is left pleading for his life and seals his own fate. Evil has a tendency to implode, and it certainly does at this moment in history: Haman is impaled by order of the king on the very pole he prepared for Mordecai.

When overwhelmed by the enormity of what we are facing, be it responsibility, antagonism or confrontation, Esther's story 'comforts' us, in the original sense of the Latin word *confortare*, meaning to greatly strengthen. If God leads us to a course of action, he will enable us to follow through. Where God guides, he provides.

Esther plays her part, and the consequences unfold in ways that she cannot possibly have imagined. There may be times when confrontation is the only way forward and we feel compelled to call a situation out honestly and courageously, whether in public life or private life, while unsure of the outcome and the personal cost. Esther reminds us that God is always committed to justice and to his people.

Lord, grant us strength to speak out against injustice. Amen.

FIONA STATTA

Friday 4 July   **Esther 8:11; 9:22 (NLT, abridged)**

Deliverance

The king's decree gave the Jews in every city authority to unite to defend their lives. They were allowed to kill, slaughter, and annihilate anyone of any nationality or province who might attack them or their children and wives, and to take the property of their enemies… [Mordecai] told them to celebrate… with feasting and gladness and by giving gifts of food to each other and presents to the poor. This would commemorate a time when the Jews gained relief from their enemies, when their sorrow was turned into gladness and their mourning into joy.

No Persian law could be revoked, for kings were regarded as deity; but another law could neutralise its impact, making it difficult to implement. Mordecai is asked to write a new decree in the king's name. In his God-given wisdom, Mordecai places limits on the actions the Judahites may take: they are only permitted to defend themselves when attacked. Meanwhile, Mordecai's reputation grows so exponentially that many in high positions give him their allegiance. Indeed, in some parts of the Persian kingdom, no stand is taken against the Judahites, and many expediently adopt their faith. In these ways bloodshed is reduced and limited to those who openly oppose God's people in Susa and beyond.

Although taking property from their enemies is sanctioned by Mordecai, no plunder is actually taken. Restraint is shown. Nevertheless, it is a tragedy that Haman's open abhorrence of Mordecai's race, expressed at the highest level in the empire, incites his sons and many other Persians to hatred, resulting in conflict and bloodshed. God in his sovereignty delivers his people. We follow him in opposing all racial prejudice and injustice.

Sorrow is turned to gladness and mourning to joy as they celebrate their deliverance. This language is evocative of the prophet's words in Isaiah 61, which point to a greater deliverer, the long-awaited Messiah. Jesus identifies himself as fulfilling this prophecy. Mordecai's and Esther's deliverance of their people foreshadow Jesus' world-embracing deliverance from sin and death.

Lord, deliver us! Give us a crown of beauty instead of ashes, the oil of joy instead of mourning and a garment of praise instead of a spirit of despair. May we be like strong oaks planted for your glory (Isaiah 61:3). Amen.

FIONA STRATTA

Saturday 5 July — **Esther 9:28; 10:3 (NLT, abridged)**

Celebration and flourishing

These days would be remembered and kept from generation to generation… This Festival of Purim would never cease to be celebrated among the Jews, nor would the memory of what happened ever die out among their descendants… Mordecai the Jew became the prime minister, with authority next to that of King Xerxes himself. He was very great among the Jews, who held him in high esteem, because he continued to work for the good of his people and to speak up for the welfare of all their descendants.

Purim is still celebrated and is accompanied by retelling Esther's story; a play may be performed, often humorously, making the most of the dramatic ironies within the narrative. The customs continue: dressing up, feasting within the community and giving gifts both to friends and to the poor. This reminds us of the importance of not forgetting the needy when we celebrate.

Throughout the Bible, remembering and celebrating through festivals are part of the way of life ordained by God for his people. They continue to be part of our faith journey, through the Eucharist and the rhythm of Christian festivals in which we remember Jesus' birth, death, resurrection and ascension, as well as the coming of the Holy Spirit. Celebrating with friends and family often becomes all the more poignant in dark and difficult times. It uplifts and comforts us, encouraging us to remain hopeful and enabling joy to emerge. Godly celebration does us good – body, mind and soul – as we share with loved ones and reflect on the goodness of God. These celebrations foreshadow the great wedding feast at Christ's return, when there will be no more death, mourning or pain.

Our final look at Mordecai, now prime minister, sees him using his position to work for the good of the people, including the welfare of the young and of future generations. These are hallmarks of a good leader and ones to look for when choosing leaders in our churches, communities and countries. Mordecai inspires us to live a life focussed on blessing those around us.

Lord, may we know your shalom (peace) as we work for the flourishing of others wherever you place us. May we celebrate your faithfulness and trust in your sovereignty (Jeremiah 29:7). Amen.

FIONA STRATTA

Introduction

Peacemaking

'Blessed are the peacemakers, for they will be called children of God' (Matthew 5:9, NRSV) is the only verse in the Bible where the word 'peacemaker' is used. However, there are many examples of what it means to be a peacemaker found throughout the Bible.

Peacemaking is celebrated not just in the Bible, but by society in general. Each year, the Nobel Peace Prize is given to a person or people who have been exemplary in working towards peace among nations or communities in that year. Meanwhile the United Nations has set aside 21 September each year as the International Day of Peace, when it is hoped that peace can be strengthened and celebrated through the laying down of arms for 24 hours.

Peace is a yearning of the human heart. When we see and hear about the bloodshed and wars around us, something deep inside us cries out for peace. We are aware of the tainted and broken nature of ourselves as well as of the creation of which we are part. We have a sense that things are not the way they are supposed to be. We are right: the world is broken. The world is broken by selfishness, greed and the evil within our hearts: by sin.

Nevertheless as Christians we are not without hope, nor is our heart-cry for peace unanswered. Jesus is called the 'Prince of Peace' (Isaiah 9:6), and in turn he calls those who choose to follow him and count themselves as children of God to be peacemakers.

Biblical peacemaking, however, is not an avoidance of conflict or a glossing over of issues. Instead, biblical peacemakers run towards the problems and face them head-on in order to bring about reconciliation between the people involved and God, and also with each other.

Over the coming seven days, join me as we explore what it means to be a peacemaker and how we can effectively live out this calling. We will meet people from a variety of backgrounds in both the Old and New Testaments and see how peacemaking can be applied in a variety of ways.

As we journey together, may you be filled with the peace of God which passes understanding and may your heart and eyes be opened to what God is teaching you about peacemaking with the people and within the communities where you live today.

MATT MCCHLERY

Sunday 6 July   **1 Samuel 25:34–35 (NRSV)**

Abigail

'For as surely as the Lord the God of Israel lives, who has restrained me from hurting you, unless you had hurried and come to meet me, truly by morning there would not have been left to Nabal so much as one male.' Then David received from her hand what she had brought him; he said to her, 'Go up to your house in peace; see, I have heeded your voice, and I have granted your petition.'

Today's Bible passage is taken from a larger story of a remarkable woman who embodied what it means to be a peacemaker.

We begin with 1 Samuel 25, in which we are introduced to Nabal, a rich yet unkind man. Previously David's men had been good to Nabal's shepherds and flocks that were grazing nearby. David now found himself in need, so he sent a messenger to ask Nabal for some provisions. Mean-hearted, Nabal denies David's request, ruining the previously good relationship. David, along with 400 of his men set off to fight Nabal.

Luckily for Nabal, one of his servants told his wife Abigail what had happened. Abigail immediately gathers some provisions and loads up several donkeys with them and sets off to meet David. When she finds David, she falls on her face before him and begs for his forgiveness. She asks him to change his mind and spare their lives.

David is grateful to Abigail for her 'good sense' (v. 33) and is pleased she has been able to convince him not to spill the blood of guiltless men that day. He turns back and Abigail goes in peace, the crisis averted.

I admire Abigail for taking the brave step of seeking out a very angry David, who was on the warpath. She could not have known if her petition would have made a difference, but she made the effort to try to bring about a resolution anyway. Sometimes, like Abigail, we need to be brave enough to speak the truth even when circumstances around us are unpleasant or dangerous.

Jesus, help me to be brave in difficult circumstances. Help me to speak the truth in love even if this may result in unpleasant consequences. Amen.

MATT MCCHLERY

Monday 7 July   **Jonah 3:3–5 (NRSV)**

Jonah

Jonah set out and went to Nineveh, according to the word of the Lord. Now Nineveh was an exceedingly large city, a three days' walk across. Jonah began to go into the city, going a day's walk. And he cried out, 'Forty days more, and Nineveh shall be overthrown!' And the people of Nineveh believed God; they proclaimed a fast, and everyone, great and small, put on sackcloth.

Has God asked you to do something that you really did not want to do? He has asked me to do so, which leads me to ponder whether the tension between fear and obedience play a part in peacemaking.

Jonah was a reluctant and angry peacemaker. He did not want Nineveh to repent, but rather to be destroyed. At the time it was a powerful enemy to Israel. We can understand Jonah's reluctance to go and inform that city of its impending doom. He was probably afraid they would kill him. Yet equally he also knew the nature of God and was aware that his prophetic word might turn the hearts of those in Nineveh towards God, and that God would not destroy them after all.

We see how his fear and hatred of his enemies led him to run away from the purposes of God and this landed him in a heap of trouble inside a big fish. He repented and agreed to obey and then delivered the word of God to the city of Nineveh, despite his misgivings.

Unsurprisingly, as the hearts of the people were redirected towards God, they realised the error of their ways and repented. God's wrath was turned away and forgiveness was extended. Peace had been made. Jonah did a good job, although he regretted it and still got angry about it.

Peacemaking may involve us taking risks. It includes us reconciling people with God and allowing the Holy Spirit to work within the situation. It may even mean we need to come alongside people we may not necessarily like. Let us do so with a good attitude, unlike Jonah.

Jesus, help me not to be an angry peacemaker. Help me to follow your leading and to live the way you have asked me to even among people I may not agree with. Amen.

MATT MCCHLERY

Tuesday 8 July   **Philippians 4:1–3 (NRSV)**

Euodia and Syntyche

Therefore, my brothers and sisters, whom I love and long for, my joy and crown, stand firm in the Lord in this way, my beloved. I urge Euodia and I urge Syntyche to be of the same mind in the Lord. Yes, and I ask you also, my loyal companion, help these women, for they have struggled beside me in the work of the gospel, together with Clement and the rest of my coworkers, whose names are in the book of life.

If you have been part of a church for any length of time you will know that disagreements happen. Sadly, even within the church there can be friction and people can fall out with each other. I have experienced the pain of this myself.

In his letter to the Philippians, Paul addresses a relationship problem that has occurred between two women, Euodia and Syntyche. We do not know the cause, but we know it was serious enough for Paul to address it directly.

Paul urges both women to seek out the mind of the Lord, and not merely hold fast to their position of who is right or wrong. Seeking the mind of the Lord is a good idea whenever we find ourselves at odds with a fellow believer. It is always a good idea to bring the person with whom we are disagreeing to the Lord in prayer, as it can not only change the person we are praying for, but also ourselves.

Paul is being a long-distance peacemaker, not ignoring issues that need to be sorted out but encouraging believers in that community to confront and deal with them. However, there is also another peacemaker in this example. Paul appoints his 'loyal companion' to help these women settle their dispute and to mediate and help bring about reconciliation and healing. We may also benefit from an outside party helping us when we are finding it difficult to reconcile with a brother or sister in Christ. Or indeed, we may find that we are the ones being the loyal companion, helping others to come to a resolution.

Jesus, help me to resolve issues I may have with others in my church quickly, not brushing things under the carpet. Help me to do so in a kind and loving way. Amen.

MATT MCCHLERY

Wednesday 9 July — Acts 15:1–2 (NRSV)

Paul and Barnabas

Then certain individuals came down from Judea and were teaching the brothers, 'Unless you are circumcised according to the custom of Moses, you cannot be saved.' And after Paul and Barnabas had no small dissension and debate with them, Paul and Barnabas and some of the others were appointed to go up to Jerusalem to discuss this question with the apostles and the elders.

Have you noticed the trend in our culture today, where everyone is apparently entitled to their own opinion so long as it matches the opinion most widely held by those in our society? Dissenting voices are shouted at so loudly they are drowned out and others are afraid to speak against things they see as wrong to keep the peace.

Keeping quiet to keep the peace is not what being a peacemaker is about. Paul and Barnabas debated long and hard in what seemed to be a heated discussion with those who were insisting that the Gentile believers should be circumcised. They could have disagreed and simply cut off ties with the Jewish elements of the church – 'We will do it our own way and refuse to listen to you!' But this would not have solved anything.

Instead, we see Paul and Barnabas, despite their strong opinions, travelling to Jerusalem to speak with the church leaders about what the correct course of action should be – even if it contradicted their opinions. We see later, in Acts 15, that this was not an easy problem to solve. The church leaders met, discussed and had much debate over the question. Eventually they decided that it was not necessary for the Gentile Christians to be circumcised, so sent word back to them of their decision. This was met with much rejoicing. Peace had been restored between the Gentile and Jewish branches of the church.

We need to learn how to disagree agreeably. This may include heated debate, but ultimately we need to be asking Jesus what his will is in any given situation and then be prepared to surrender our strong opinions to follow his leading and direction.

Jesus, help me to disagree agreeably. Give me a heart that is willing to learn and to change if it needs to, not insisting that I'm always right. Amen.

MATT MCCHLERY

Thursday 10 July   **Matthew 1:19–20, 24–25 (NRSV)**

Joseph

Her husband Joseph, being a righteous man and unwilling to expose her to public disgrace, planned to dismiss her quietly. But just when he had resolved to do this, an angel of the Lord appeared to him in a dream… When Joseph awoke from sleep, he did as the angel of the Lord commanded him; he took her as his wife but had no marital relations with her until she had given birth to a son.

The role Joseph plays in the nativity is somewhat underrated. It is true that he did not physically father Jesus, as Joseph 'had no marital relations with her until she had given birth to a son' (v. 25). So why is his role important? It is because he was a peacemaker in as much as he brought peace to Mary, who was carrying Jesus in her womb.

We should not underestimate the difficult and dangerous situation Mary found herself in when she discovered she was pregnant while being unmarried. In ancient Israel, according to the Old Testament law, unmarried women who were engaged and had sexual relations with someone to whom they were not betrothed were to be stoned to death (see Deuteronomy 22).

In the first instance, when Joseph learned that Mary was pregnant with a child he had not fathered, he decided not to expose her to public disgrace, which could lead to her execution. Instead, he kindly decided to break off their relationship and engagement quietly. This could work, and Mary might be able to escape with her life and the life of her unborn child, although this was not guaranteed.

Then there was some divine intervention. An angel delivered a message to Joseph in a dream and told him not to go through with his plan, but to marry Mary, as the child she was carrying was conceived of the Holy Spirit and that this child would save his people from their sins. By this Joseph began to understand the redemptive purpose of Jesus and that he had a part to play in helping him to fulfil it. This began with Joseph bringing peace to Mary and rescuing her from her situation.

Jesus, help us to obey you even when we may not understand why. Help us to be kind. Help us to be obedient to your leading. Amen.

MATT MCCHLERY

Friday 11 July — **Colossians 1:18–20 (NRSV)**

Jesus, Prince of Peace

He is the head of the body, the church; he is the beginning, the firstborn from the dead, so that he might come to have first place in everything. For in him all the fullness of God was pleased to dwell, and through him God was pleased to reconcile to himself all things, whether on earth or in heaven, by making peace through the blood of his cross.

In Isaiah 9:6, Jesus is described as the Prince of Peace, because he was to enable the ultimate reconciliation in all history. By his death, Jesus paid the price required by God for sin. He took on the sin of the whole world and paid the price demanded by it through his death as the only perfect and sinless human. This enabled God to be reconciled to humanity. Peace was made through the blood of his cross and the ultimate peace, the forgiveness of sin and the restoration of relationship between humanity and God, was made possible.

As Christians, peacemaking is more than just mediating between two disparate parties and helping them to resolve a conflict. It includes us pointing people to Jesus, the ultimate restorer and peacemaker. We all need to realise that our primary need is to be reconciled to God through Jesus. Then from the position of being *in* Christ, we can extend the peace and forgiveness we have received out into the brokenness and pain around us. Our restored spiritual relationship with God will enable us to far better deal with and restore broken earthly relationships.

Trying to bring about healing without involving the true healer will not produce the best result. Nor will trying to bring about peace without involving the ultimate peacemaker. We need to acknowledge that, as peacemakers, we need Jesus to be involved in the process for true and lasting peace to be completely achieved.

So whatever situation we may find ourselves in, let us come to Jesus and allow him to be actively involved in every situation. Let us allow him to lead and guide us in all of life, but especially when we are being called upon to be peacemakers.

Jesus, help us to point people to you, the only one who reconciled us with God and with each other. Amen.

MATT MCCHLERY

Saturday 12 July — Ephesians 2:14–16 (NRSV)

Jesus, our peace

For he is our peace; in his flesh he has made both into one and has broken down the dividing wall, that is, the hostility between us, abolishing the law with its commandments and ordinances, that he might create in himself one new humanity in place of the two, thus making peace, and might reconcile both to God in one body through the cross, thus putting to death that hostility through it.

Jesus is not just Prince of Peace; he *is peace* itself. The way we journey towards peace with God and with others is by moving towards Jesus. The wider context of today's passage speaks of two separate and distinct groups of people – Jews and Gentiles. There was great animosity between them. The Jewish people rightly saw themselves as the chosen people of God, and everyone else who was not Jewish, was not. They were not chosen; they were Gentiles. Jews did not trust or even deal with Gentiles. They were unclean and were to be avoided and shunned.

Here we are told that under the new covenant that Jesus brings about, the kingdom of God and being part of his family are no longer the exclusive preserve of the Jewish people but are now open to all. Jesus created a 'new humanity' that reconciled the two separate groups and made them one in Jesus. In so doing, the animosity, the distrust and hatred between them was no more – peace had come because they were now all one people, brought together into one body through the cross of Christ.

Sadly, there is still hostility between different groups of people today who distrust those they misunderstand. Divisions still exist because of social class, nationality and racial identity, among other things. But this should not be so within the church. When we are in Christ, we are all part of the same family of God – a diverse group, but one people. As we grow in Christ and come together within the body of the church, we discover that we have been reconciled with each other and that peace exists between us because Jesus *is* our peace.

Jesus, help me to continue to journey towards peace with God and with others by moving closer to you. Amen.

MATT MCCHLERY

Introduction

Psalms 67—72

Psalms 67—72 do not form a recognisable collection. Psalms 67—68 are psalms of praise and 69—71 concern the suffering of the righteous. Psalm 72 stands alone as a prayer for the king. So I shall take each psalm on its own terms, drawing out the particular approach of each text, trying to avoid repeating themes along the way when they recur.

I have often turned for a sense of the original Hebrew to Robert Alter's fine translation, *The Hebrew Bible*. John Goldingay's commentary in the Baker series has also proved a great resource. The differences in their translation, and theirs with the NRSV, are instructive because they make it apparent how many different senses can be constructed from the Hebrew text. The mood of verbs is often an issue; for example, in Psalm 67:5 is it 'Let the peoples praise you, O God' or 'Nations acclaim you, O God'?

The greatest moral challenge in this collection is the question of the enemy. In the world of the psalms, enemies exist for both the individual righteous and for the people who believe that God had chosen their nation to be holy and set apart among others. Contemporary events might make us reluctant to endorse the vehement, sometimes virulent, ways in which the psalmist enlists God for support of his/their cause.

However, there is another form of dominating the enemy to address in our own society and globally, namely, in the exchanges of social media. The weight that can so quickly fall upon individuals as they are shamed, 'cancelled' or disgraced must exceed the wildest and darkest aspirations of the psalmist for vengeance. It is not just other people who need to worry about this but all of us, because all of us are capable of seeing ourselves as righteous and of condemning others with little other than rumour and hearsay to guide our judgements.

Ending with Psalm 72 may help us to keep the big picture in mind: neither righteous nations nor individuals can live entirely for themselves. They are called to exercise justice so that even creation prospers, especially the poor. True justice cannot be blind to the needs of neighbours, even when they seem threatening. There is always a shared humanity to discover under the rule of the one and only God.

ROLAND RIEM

Sunday 13 July   **Psalm 67:1–3, 6–7 (NRSV)**

May God bless us

May God be gracious to us and bless us and make his face to shine upon us, that your way may be known upon earth, your saving power among all nations. Let the peoples praise you, O God; let all the peoples praise you… The earth has yielded its increase; God, our God, has blessed us. May God continue to bless us; let all the ends of the earth revere him.

Who is the 'us'? That's a good question to ask of any psalm. The 'us' in Psalm 67 seems inclusive enough; its meaning is never pinned down. The psalm is also a song, and in songs even intimate pronouns can hold wide reference. When we sing together 'O love that will not let *me* go', we are giving thanks for a personal yet universal embrace.

So it is here. The 'us' in the first verse begins as particular; it is borne on the praises of Israel, one small nation among many. And yet the 'us' envisaged in this worship is a dynamic, expanding confessional community. This is because Israel's God is the one true God who wishes to show his saving power among all nations and among all peoples. This small nation worships a great God.

In praise, as the vision of God's reign unfolds to the hearts and minds of those gathered, the people are invited to acknowledge that the God whose favour they seek is the one who wishes to favour all peoples. The invitation is broad, by no means confined to those who have already answered it.

And this range of blessing is evident too because of the earth, which has yielded its increase. Creation is reliably fruitful for everyone, not only for those who already glorify God. And to God's blessing of fruitfulness this psalm, in verses not quoted above, adds further evidence of God's universal favour, in the political blessings of fairness and good governance.

The psalm ends with a note of assurance that God will bless God's people, but that even the ends of the earth will one day confess this same beneficent reach.

Thank you, gracious God, that we are not the last of your people, but among the first to praise your name. Amen.

ROLAND RIEM

Monday 14 July   **Psalm 68:1–3 (NRSV)**

The God who rises up

Let God rise up; let his enemies be scattered; let those who hate him flee before him. As smoke is driven away, so drive them away; as wax melts before the fire, let the wicked perish before God. But let the righteous be joyful; let them exult before God; let them be jubilant with joy.

Christians look to the Hebrew scriptures, 'The Old Testament', as the first witness to our faith in God. If we call the Testament 'old', it is in the sense of its being foundational. The acts of Christ and his apostles change what the building of faith looks like above ground, but this structure still rests on what lies below – the life and worship of Israel. Without these foundations, the building could not stand.

The idea that God can rise up and act is foundational to Christian faith. In this psalm the hope is for God to bring victory over enemies. It may have been written in two stages, with today's verses and the closing verses of 33–35 wrapped around a much earlier psalm (verses 4–32). It is possible that a psalm celebrating a specific historic victory in battle has grown into a psalm asking God to continue victories like this: Let God arise and let his enemies be scattered!

The rising up here may refer to the ark of the covenant being lifted up and moved, as it was carried into battle bringing terror and ultimately defeat to the Philistines (1 Samuel 4). The ark embodied God's continuing presence with his people. Wherever the ark was, there God was pleased to dwell. Wherever the ark was taken, there God's presence would move, scattering his enemies 'as wax melts before the fire' (v. 2).

This holy power made 'the righteous' exult, while 'the wicked' would flee from it as if dispersed like smoke on the wind. This power could divide the bad from the good, destroying the former and raising the latter peoples, a confidence borne of a long history of God saving those who call upon his name.

God rises up to save the godly. We know this through history and, supremely, in the resurrection of Jesus Christ from the dead.

Lord, bring a victory by which you raise up the godly
and melt away evil like wax. Amen.

ROLAND RIEM

Tuesday 15 July — **Psalm 68:4–6 (NRSV)**

God of many names

Sing to God; sing praises to his name; lift up a song to him who rides upon the clouds – his name is the Lord – be exultant before him. Father of orphans and protector of widows is God in his holy habitation. God gives the desolate a home to live in; he leads out the prisoners to prosperity, but the rebellious live in a parched land.

We are used to praising God in the way in which this passage begins and are used to using many names to do justice to the manifold ways in which God has revealed himself. This is something we share with Judaism, as well as Islam, which famously lists 99 names for God.

Because the names of our own tradition are so familiar, we rarely stop to ponder how each differs from the others. The God who rides upon the clouds is linked here to a very ancient Canaanite name Yah, translated here as 'the Lord', whose name we praise every time we say 'Hallelu-jah'. It conjures an image of God whose voice bellows thunderously and who ranges over the clouds.

It is the genius of this psalm to link this idea of unbridled, celestial power to a more compassionate insight. The God who strides over the heavens is also defender of the poor on earth. He has a tender eye for orphans and widows, those with no strength to help themselves.

God needs a mighty power to protect these little ones and give them a home because many would ignore and override their needs. The fate of those who rebel against God's good ordering of society is clear. They will end up parched, while those whom God protects will be showered with blessings.

As hearts and minds are stretched in the praise of God, these two aspects of God's character, and many others, are fused. This is not only because worship is an act of expansive imagination, as we strain to see God's coming rule, but also because the church is an assembly of already-present hope. It includes and cherishes the marginalised among its members because it is called to anticipate the holy habitation to come.

God, may my church be a refuge for the defenceless, anticipating your final victory over those who rebel against you. Amen.

ROLAND RIEM

Wednesday 16 July   **Psalm 68:7–10 (NRSV)**

God provides

O God, when you went out before your people, when you marched through the wilderness, the earth quaked, the heavens poured down rain at the presence of God, the God of Sinai, at the presence of God, the God of Israel. Rain in abundance, O God, you showered abroad; you restored your heritage when it languished; your flock found a dwelling in it; in your goodness, O God, you provided for the needy.

There were hints in yesterday's verses about the event which most shaped the people's understanding of God as deliverer, their liberation from Egypt. There God was described as 'the one who leads out the prisoners [or captives] to prosperity' (v. 6). The story moves on to the wilderness wandering, where God guided them by a pillar of cloud by day and a pillar of fire by night. He marched ahead and the liberated followed.

The God of Sinai is invoked in this remembrance, the one who, having brought his people out of Egypt and through the wilderness, gave the people the law to bind them together as a holy people. The deliverance from Egypt and the giving of the commandments proved in their different ways that God's acts were always for their good. Looking back on their sacred history, therefore, the people praised God for his mighty acts to restore their heritage.

It is also important for us to rehearse this sacred history, as we recall it in worship and in the scriptures, because the daily analysis of the secular media assumes that events happen without God. Economic, psychological and social mechanisms undoubtedly play their part but do not admit the ultimate action of God in, through and beyond these processes.

So we remind ourselves that we are the sheep of God's flock whom he wants to lead by obedience into good pastures. God promises the liberation of a people who know their need and know who meets it. The forceful words of Jesus, when he declares that he is the gate for the sheep and the good shepherd, return us to the ancient assurance that God's loving kindness is towards all those who fear him.

God our provider, help us to trust that your power is for us,
ready to deliver us as we put our trust in you. Amen.

ROLAND RIEM

Thursday 17 July   **Psalm 68:11–14 (NRSV)**

A dove spoiled

The Lord gives the command; great is the company of [the women] who bore the tidings: 'The kings of the armies, they flee, they flee!' The women at home divide the spoil, though they stay among the sheepfolds – the wings of a dove covered with silver, its pinions with green gold. When the Almighty scattered kings there, snow fell on Zalmon.

Psalm 68 includes a long section describing a triumphal procession after a decisive military victory, in the area now called the Golan Heights. It contains difficult verses, wishing the worst possible harm to befall enemies and rejoicing that this once captive people can now celebrate the humiliation of others taken captive in battle.

Today's verses, which anticipate that victory march, are easier to take devotionally because of their Christian resonance. The ones who bring the good news of victory in the New Testament are called evangelists, borrowing the idea of messengers running ahead bearing the glad tidings of triumph.

In the victory preparations, the women take the lead. This company of evangelists is female. It is the women at home who divide up the spoil of battle. These and previous verses recall the Song of Deborah, which celebrates how Deborah bravely rid Israel of Sisera, the commander of the Canaanite army (Judges 5).

Missing words in sources of this portion mean that we cannot be sure of the connection of these preparations to the beautiful object described, the wings of a dove inlaid with silver and her pinions with green, or precious, gold. Possibly this was part of the booty of war. If so, it is a timely reminder that the enemies brought low by Israel had their own cultural treasures, which, in the heat of battle and the joy of victory, were seen as spoils.

The object was a dove. Though this could have been a representation of the Canaanite mother goddess Asherah, the dove became a symbol of Israel itself, and for Christians a symbol of God's intimate presence and anointing. The stock of natural symbols is shared by humanity and reused in different ways to point beyond the natural realm to core beliefs and values.

Holy Spirit, gentle dove, show us the way to peace, not plunder, and open our hearts to cultures beyond our own. Amen.

ROLAND RIEM

Friday 18 July — Psalm 68:32–35 (NRSV)

God unconfined

Sing to God, O kingdoms of the earth; sing praises to the Lord, O rider in the heavens, the ancient heavens; listen, he sends out his voice, his mighty voice. Ascribe power to God, whose majesty is over Israel and whose power is in the skies. Awesome is God in his sanctuary, the God of Israel; he gives power and strength to his people. Blessed be God!

These closing verses of Psalm 68 are a song of praise, connected to the verses before it by the theme of power. It is God's power that has won a victory over the nations and led to a solemn procession to the temple, and it is God's power evident in creation, in the skies shared by other nations, who also hear the thunder of his voice.

The psalm's military imagery made it the favourite psalm of the warrior-king Charlemagne, the first emperor of the Holy Roman Empire. Its language can easily be used to justify 'shattering the heads' of the enemy. In this context it is especially important to realise that, while Israel is called to belong exclusively to the Lord, the Lord does not commit to belonging exclusively to Israel.

We taste this truth as we praise God. Praise strengthens the bond between worshippers and God. In praising God we confess that we belong to him, and we desire that others should join our praise. We do not know, though, how God will act to bring in the nations. It is unlikely to be by military means, even though this psalm remembers one famous instance of this.

The poetry of praise is confident and evocative, but vague: 'O rider in the heavens... he sends out his voice' (v. 33). We have a sense that the invitation which has summoned us will be offered elsewhere, because we know what a difference God has made to us: 'He gives power and strength to his people' (v. 35).

Praise leads to awe. God's majesty is 'over' Israel, and this means that those who worship him can only marvel at what they have not yet grasped of his greatness. The sanctuary is a place where God's holy power is given lodging, but where it can never be confined.

God unconfined, may we fear you, and in fearing you,
know something of your greatness. Amen.

ROLAND RIEM

Saturday 19 July   **Psalm 69:1–4 (NRSV)**

Beyond drowning

Save me, O God, for the waters have come up to my neck. I sink in deep mire, where there is no foothold; I have come into deep waters, and the flood sweeps over me. I am weary with my crying; my throat is parched. My eyes grow dim with waiting for my God. More in number than the hairs of my head are those who hate me without cause; many are those who would destroy me, my enemies who accuse me falsely. What I did not steal, must I now restore?

Drowning is a recurrent nightmare, especially when we feel in danger of being overwhelmed. The beginning of Psalm 69 is a prayer for deliverance from a threat so engulfing that only this terrifying metaphor will do. It is agonising to sense a relentless rising tide, to have just breath enough to know that further pressure will plunge our gaping mouths under the waterline.

We tend to think of death as the point at which our life ends. The Hebrew understanding, however, was that life and death lay on a continuum. Death could suddenly suck you down into the pit of darkness, whether by physical illness or mental distress. The ground beneath a human being could become quicksand.

Today's drowning is being caused by how others are treating the complainant. He cannot understand why a multitude has turned against him, when he has done nothing to provoke them. He has been falsely accused of stealing. He feels the pressure to meet their lies by giving back what he never stole. He is hoarse from crying out to God, and his eyes fail from scanning the horizon for hope.

This psalm reflects what it feels like to have the stuffing knocked out of you by the prejudice and hostility of others, and the sense that prayer is useless. The fact that the psalm continues is a testament to what faith means. How it continues will show us how to pray when despair and disorientation dominate and our worst and best thought is to drown and die.

Have I ever given up too soon on God's rescue from 'drowning'?
What has happened when I have persisted?

ROLAND RIEM

Sunday 20 July   **Psalm 69:5–9 (NRSV)**

Guilt and grief

O God, you know my folly; the wrongs I have done are not hidden from you. Do not let those who hope in you be put to shame because of me, O Lord God of hosts; do not let those who seek you be dishonoured because of me, O God of Israel. It is for your sake that I have borne reproach, that shame has covered my face. I have become a stranger to my kindred, an alien to my mother's children. It is zeal for your house that has consumed me; the insults of those who insult you have fallen on me.

The drowning one continues with God. We may not have been surprised if he had lashed out at his persecutors or protested his innocence. Instead, he confesses his guilt, perhaps because of the belief that his misfortune resulted from God's displeasure.

This belief is found in one strand of the biblical tradition (the Deuteronomistic), but it is challenged elsewhere, such as where Job argues against his accusers that, whatever they might believe about his guilt before God, he has done nothing to justify the catastrophe befalling him.

This confession of guilt relieves the psalmist of the need to justify himself. Even if he is not a thief, he cannot stand defiant. He worries that he will be a stumbling block to others who, like him, seek God – that he might put his fellow seekers off. This absence of self-absorption is a sign that, even in despair, he remains on the right track.

Closer to home, the psalmist finds scorn from others and alienation from his own kin. 'Zeal for your house' (v. 9) has caused this, possibly meaning a zeal to rebuild the temple destroyed during the exile in Babylon, a course of action that strongly divided the community returning to Judah. Even if zeal proved the psalmist's fierce allegiance to God, it brought him no peace.

As he is dragged down into the realm of death in the following verses, all the psalmist can do is grieve and do the things expected – fasting, weeping, putting on sackcloth. His piety cannot protect him from the raw feelings of being alienated from family, friends and the community of the faithful.

Lord, deliver those lost in guilt or locked in grief. Amen.

ROLAND RIEM

Monday 21 July   **Psalm 69:18–21 (NRSV)**

Forsaken but faithful

Draw near to me; redeem me; set me free because of my enemies. You know the insults I receive and my shame and dishonour; my foes are all known to you. Insults have broken my heart, so that I am in despair. I looked for pity, but there was none; and for comforters, but I found none. They gave me poison for food, and for my thirst they gave me vinegar to drink.

In Matthew's gospel, when Jesus utters his words of abandonment from the cross, someone runs to fetch a sponge with sour wine and offers it to him on a stick (Matthew 27:48) – one of many things that happen to Jesus 'according to the scriptures' as he approaches crucifixion. Matthew wanted his readers to understand that God was in charge, bringing prophecy to fulfilment, despite outward appearances.

Yet there is more than this going on. Many of the scriptures cited are from the Psalms and are used to explore the meaning of prophetic suffering. Being offered sour wine to drink is the very opposite of kindness – an absence of sympathy, rather scorn; an absence of comfort, rather cruelty.

The psalmist is broken by his own people turning on him. They might have ignored his plight, but instead they celebrate it. They kick him while he is down and because he is down. Under this intolerable weight of hatred, the psalmist prays for retribution on his enemies: 'Let them be blotted out of the book of the living; let them not be enrolled among the righteous' (v. 28). This is an understandable and honest way of praying, but it reminds us yet again of how extraordinary was Jesus' silence on the cross in his forsakenness; it did not turn to retribution against his enemies.

The psalmist keeps the faith, maintaining that God knows the insults he receives. When we pray we do so in the faith that God is still involved with us, caring about injustice, even without sight of God's redemption. If the psalmist prays for retribution, he does not take retribution upon himself but leaves it to God, who knows and understands the terrible plight that he suffers.

If I cannot keep silent when forsaken, help me, Lord, to leave vengeance to you; for you are just and forgiving. Amen.

ROLAND RIEM

Tuesday 22 July   **Psalm 69:29–33 (NRSV)**

From pain to praise

But I am lowly and in pain; let your salvation, O God, protect me. I will praise the name of God with a song; I will magnify him with thanksgiving. This will please the Lord more than an ox or a bull with horns and hoofs. Let the oppressed see it and be glad; you who seek God, let your hearts revive. For the Lord hears the needy and does not despise his own who are in bonds.

Praying is rarely a tidy process, even though the prayers used in formal worship have a polish to them which may give that impression. Scholars who have divided the psalms into various 'forms' quickly conclude that many forms are mixed, such as where a psalm of lament turns suddenly into a psalm of praise.

This might be because an individual writer's supplications to God were interrupted by an unexpected twist of fortune. Or it may be because different sorts of literature were brought together over time to form a composite psalm expressing a broad range of emotion. All we have now is the text.

From the very first verse, the psalmist is asking God for personal deliverance. The line 'I am in distress – make haste to answer me' (v. 17) summarises the whole psalm, a long prayer asking for something to change to make someone's life bearable. This finally happens. The plot of the text, therefore, is of an answered prayer.

We are not told what has changed, how prayer has been answered, but we hear its unmistakable sound in praise. The perspective that does not change is that God is the one who delivers and God is the one to be thanked for deliverance. The psalmist has persisted with praying, despite all the counter evidence, because he has been sure of the character of God: the Lord hears the needy and does not despise his captive people.

The song of thanksgiving is offered in the conviction that God will value it more than ritual sacrifice, and that it will encourage those who saw the psalmist's plight earlier and who, as he worried then, might have been put off seeking God by seeing his previous misery.

When prayer has been answered, was there a warning?
Did grace dawn slowly or did it suddenly amaze?

ROLAND RIEM

Wednesday 23 July — Psalm 70:1–4 (NRSV)

Make haste to help me

Be pleased, O God, to deliver me. O Lord, make haste to help me! Let those be put to shame and confusion who seek my life. Let those be turned back and brought to dishonour who desire to hurt me. Let those who say, 'Aha, Aha!' turn back because of their shame. Let all who seek you rejoice and be glad in you. Let those who love your salvation say evermore, 'God is great!'

The opening words of this psalm were drawn into Christian worship by the fourth-century monk John Cassian, who believed that praying 'O God, make speed to save us' was a sure way to repel demons and stray thoughts. In its original context, though, the obvious problem was not spiritual warfare but enemies who threatened the wellbeing of the one praying for deliverance.

What prayer might be helpful when persecution threatens? To put it in Cassian's language, what prayer will stop the devil from entering our hearts?

The first thing to note is that prayer should not turn our hearts to violence. We may well harbour negative thoughts against others, but the overall intention of our prayer should be God's salvation for the ones besieged rather than seeking to bring down harm on others' heads. When we use prayers like these it is easy to believe that we are entirely right and enlightened, while the enemies at our gate are wrong and blind to truth. We may well believe this when first smarting from our wounds, but this perspective in the longer term cannot lead to reconciliation.

Second, this psalm offers to God the realm of inward intention and desire, which is a hard and hidden landscape to read, both in ourselves and in others. However much we suffer from others' actions towards us, we would do well to allow God to do the saving and God to read the secrets of all our hearts.

We hope that even our enemies might long for the same salvation for which we pray, and that God's deliverance would embrace them also. The closing verse of the psalm is the best path.

'But I am poor and needy; hasten to me, O God! You are my help and my deliverer; O Lord, do not delay!' (v. 5). Amen.

ROLAND RIEM

Thursday 24 July   **Psalm 72:1–4 (NRSV)**

The ideal king

Give the king your justice, O God, and your righteousness to a king's son. May he judge your people with righteousness and your poor with justice. May the mountains yield prosperity for the people, and the hills, in righteousness. May he defend the cause of the poor of the people, give deliverance to the needy, and crush the oppressor.

This psalm could offer messianic hope, imagining a future to come but not yet present, but it is more probably a description of what an ideal king should be like now. The title of the psalm looks back nostalgically to Solomon son of David as such a king, despite the long list of his errors recorded in 1 Kings 11.

The psalm opens with a prayer for the king, for his exercise of righteous judgement to tilt the balance of justice towards the lowly and away from those who oppress them. This is a principle held in our democracy whatever its political persuasion, because it is taken for granted by all parties that opportunity and wealth carry responsibility. The blend of these in practice might be at issue, but the underlying moral vision never is.

The vision here is not simply that righteous government will raise up the least well off and least powerful; it is rather that it will make a difference to the whole ecology of creation. No causal connection between the human realm and the mountainous regions is given, but the psalm conveys the conviction that the impact of righteousness will reach far further than the bounds of human transaction. Somehow the whole ecosystem is rebalanced when justice holds sway.

One way to imagine this connection is in the allocation of natural resources. A just system today must include how water, air and land are treated as for the common good, so that, for example, a few must not become rich at the expense of others who suffer the effects of pollution downwind or downstream. It is certainly right and just for there to be laws preventing the exploitation of these resources without heed to consequences that the rich and powerful find easier to avoid.

---

*Have we a vision for exercising justice in society
which includes bringing harmony to creation?*

ROLAND RIEM

Friday 25 July   **Psalm 72:5–9 (NRSV)**

What prosperity feels like

May he live while the sun endures and as long as the moon, throughout all generations. May he be like rain that falls on the mown grass, like showers that water the earth. In his days may righteousness flourish and peace abound, until the moon is no more. May he have dominion from sea to sea and from the River to the ends of the earth. May his foes bow down before him, and his enemies lick the dust.

Prosperity has little to do with money; it is the deep-seated feeling we have of being able to flourish. As our prospering depends on finding the right conditions in which to grow, the language of the psalm turns again to natural metaphors.

Mowing grass encourages it to grow back thickly but at the cost of momentarily damaging the blades, which release their characteristic scent as a distress signal. Mown grass needs rain as an essential nutrient to promote its growth. The king being 'like the showers that water the earth' (v. 6) is performing an equally vital function in the growth of a prosperous society.

A prospering people also need protection. We have already seen how the poor will be protected by the king's rule from their oppressors within the land; the lens now opens further to consider potential foreign oppressors. The people wish for the king's rule to dominate the surrounding powers, to give safety to them from the Dead Sea to the Mediterranean Sea and from the River Euphrates to Spain, the then outer limit of the earth.

It is hard to read this desired domination positively in the light of the tragedy that has unfolded in the Middle East, in which a state's aim of protecting itself permanently from its enemies has proved so destructive. Within the logic of the psalm, however, it is possible to imagine the king's rule as forceful but always aimed at bringing justice to the lowly.

Popular sentiment about national supremacy is often sweeping and emotive – think of the song 'Rule Britannia!' – but those who wish to rule in righteousness must do better than seeking to subjugate their national neighbours.

The first duty of any state is to protect its people, but how can this be done with righteousness across territorial borders?

ROLAND RIEM

Saturday 26 July   **Psalm 72:17–19 (NRSV)**

The king's majesty

May his name endure forever, his fame continue as long as the sun. May all nations be blessed in him; may they pronounce him happy. Blessed be the Lord, the God of Israel, who alone does wondrous things. Blessed be his glorious name forever; may his glory fill the whole earth. Amen and Amen.

The 17th-century prayer for the king's majesty is now rarely used. It asks: 'Endure him plenteously with heavenly gifts; grant him in health and wealth long to live; strengthen him that he may overcome and vanquish all his enemies; and finally, after this life, he may attain everlasting joy and felicity; through Jesus Christ our Lord.'

We may not use prayer exactly like that, but the duty of Christians to pray for those in authority remains, and we tend to do this in models that reach back to the pattern found in the Old Testament. Psalm 72 may give an idealised version of how a king reigns and of the nature and scope of the impact of righteous rule, but having an ideal in mind does no harm as we pray for our all-too-fallible leaders.

Our prayer may be helped by understanding that whatever we are praying for, the king or any in authority, we pray for because of what we ultimately believe about God. We believe that God wishes to bless all that he has made and that in blessing his creation God delights in the blessings returned to his throne. With God, creation and us, it is blessings all round – blessings for us of prosperity and peace, blessings for God in praise and thanksgiving, and blessings for creation in the flourishing of the natural order.

While sometimes in the psalms God is invoked to act in partisan ways or at least in ways that immediately favour a chosen nation, at other times, especially when the imagination of the nation is stretched by praise in corporate worship, the vision changes to all nations being blessed in him. That is why this royal and messianic tradition opens so fruitfully on to the reign of Jesus. Christ reigns in an ideal way from the cross, though we still long to receive the full blessings of his rule.

'Amen and Amen. The prayers of David son of Jesse are ended' (vv. 19–20).

ROLAND RIEM

Introduction

1 Corinthians 1—8

Corinth was a cosmopolitan city and a key trading port in the ancient world. It owed its importance to geography, for it controlled the passage of ships wanting to cross the isthmus. Think of the way that some of today's cities are marked by trade, such as New York and London. People came from far and wide and brought their cultures and religions with them. The church reflected the wide range of social structures within Corinth, from the wealthy who lived in grand villas to the casual labourers near the port and the slaves from around the empire. The gospel had to speak into all this in order to make headway, and Paul was clearly not the only person seeking to plant a church.

All this is reflected in the letter written by Paul from Ephesus to the young Corinthian church. 1 Corinthians is a practical letter which addresses specific problems that had come to Paul's attention. This is not to say that it contains no theology. Everything Paul says is grounded in his theological outlook as a preacher of the gospel of Jesus Christ, crucified and risen from the dead, and the end of the letter which is not included in this series of studies is all about the resurrection, without which the whole enterprise of believing in Jesus made no sense at all.

It seems, however, that his preaching had not been impressive enough for some who wanted a leader who exuded power and who stood out from the rest. Power is the predominant theme in the early part of 1 Corinthians, where Paul contrasts the foolishness of God with the wisdom of this world. God's power was something entirely different from anything the world had to offer, and its source lay in a crucified Messiah.

Wisdom such as this turned everything on its head and demanded a different way of living, as Paul goes on to show in the specific issues addressed in the letter. Behind the questions about the ministry of various apostles, sexual immorality, lawsuits, marriage versus singleness and food offered to idols, we can hear and imagine the factions and disputes splitting the young Corinthian church apart. It must have pained Paul deeply to be so far away at such a critical time in the life of this Christian community.

LIZ HOARE

Sunday 27 July   **1 Corinthians 1:1–5 (NRSV)**

Greetings in the Lord

Paul, called to be an apostle of Christ Jesus by the will of God, and our brother Sosthenes, To the church of God in Corinth, to those who are sanctified in Christ Jesus, called to be saints, together with all those who in every place call on the name of our Lord Jesus Christ, both their Lord and ours: Grace to you and peace from God our Father and the Lord Jesus Christ. I give thanks to my God always for you because of the grace of God that has been given you in Christ Jesus, for in every way you have been enriched in him, in speech and knowledge of every kind.

Paul always began his letters with a greeting. His reference to his apostleship in verse 1 will be an important matter as the letter develops and his reference to the Christians of Corinth as 'those who are sanctified' and 'called to be saints' (v. 2) are phrases that apply to all of us who are followers of Jesus Christ. We too have received 'grace… and peace from God our Father and the Lord Jesus Christ' (v. 3). It is worth pondering these wonderful truths of who we are in Christ as we begin this letter and discover the complicated situation in the Corinthian church.

Our human weakness and frailty trip us up at times, but no matter how much we fail, if we are Christ's, he is determined to hold us fast and complete what he has begun in us. As these opening words demonstrate, it is all because of Jesus, not because of anything we have done or failed to do.

In the first nine verses, Paul mentions Jesus eight times. Even though Paul will have some hard things to say in the course of the letter, he is above all thankful to God for calling them into his grace-filled embrace. He is therefore confident that it will be God's faithfulness that will keep them to the very end (v. 8).

Loving Lord, I thank you for the grace lavished on me as your child. Help me to receive that grace again today with open hands and heart. Amen.

LIZ HOARE

Monday 28 July   **1 Corinthians 1:10–13 (NRSV)**

A divided community

Now I appeal to you, brothers and sisters, by the name of our Lord Jesus Christ, that all of you be in agreement and that there should be no divisions among you but that you be knit together in the same mind and the same purpose. For it has been made clear to me by Chloe's people that there are quarrels among you, my brothers and sisters. What I mean is that each of you says, 'I belong to Paul', or 'I belong to Apollos', or 'I belong to Cephas', or 'I belong to Christ'. Has Christ been divided? Was Paul crucified for you? Or were you baptised in the name of Paul?

Paul dives straight in to tackle head-on the problems in the church at Corinth. News had reached him that there were divisions within the church. Factions, at root, are about who is 'in' and who is 'out', which is an immediate negation of the warm, all-inclusive nature of Paul's initial greeting.

How could this have happened? Corinth, lying as it did at a major crossroads of the ancient world and visited by people from many different nations and cultures, was also visited by various evangelists and apostles. Paul was not the only one to have preached the gospel of Jesus Christ to the people of Corinth, and it seems that he and his message were being rated in comparison to others who were perhaps more impressive orators. While some were content to identify with Paul, others chose a different allegiance and there was even a group that tried to trump all the rest by claiming they followed Christ!

Unfortunately, such comparisons arise just as easily in the church today. It might begin with a friendly 'critique' of a visiting preacher's sermon or an unfavourable comparison between different groups: which is more important, the prayer group or the music group, for example? It is never right to play one church leader or group off against another in this way within the body of Christ.

Loving God, I echo Paul's prayer that you would heal divisions within your church and unite us in Jesus. Amen.

LIZ HOARE

Tuesday 29 July   **1 Corinthians 1:26–29 (NRSV)**

God's upside-down wisdom

Consider your own call, brothers and sisters: not many of you were wise by human standards, not many were powerful, not many were of noble birth. But God chose what is foolish in the world to shame the wise; God chose what is weak in the world to shame the strong; God chose what is low and despised in the world, things that are not, to abolish things that are, so that no one might boast in the presence of God.

One of the beautiful consequences of turning to Christ is the realisation that we are precious in his sight for no other reason than being created by God. Wealth, status, IQ or any human qualification does not alter our worth in God's eyes. We are beloved simply for who we are. This is not the way of the world, where wealth, status, birth and so many other human achievements bring power in their wake along with a sense of entitlement.

In truth, Paul argues, God deliberately chooses those whom the world looks down on in order to correct the relationships between human beings so that we value one another as God does. He is not saying that God has actively caused some to have to struggle in life just so that those who expect to do well are shamed into doing deeds of charity. But he is reminding this disunited church that none of them can claim superiority over another at the foot of the cross.

It is a lesson we have to learn over and over again. Jesus told stories about people who expected to have the best seats at the table, to be shown honour and respect or who earned the right to a good lifestyle, all on their own merits. Not so, insists Paul; we are called to live differently and not only to stand against the tide of human boasting, but to find ways of actively turning it around. How might we do this in our churches, not with mere tokens, but real instances of choosing to make room for the weak, the poor and the overlooked?

Take time to listen to the story of someone in your church who is not a leader.

LIZ HOARE

Wednesday 30 July   **1 Corinthians 2:1–5 (NRSV)**

Nothing but Jesus Christ crucified

When I came to you, brothers and sisters, I did not come proclaiming the testimony of God to you with superior speech or wisdom. For I decided to know nothing among you except Jesus Christ and him crucified. And I came to you in weakness and in fear and in much trembling. My speech and my proclamation were made not with persuasive words of wisdom but with a demonstration of the Spirit and of power, so that your faith might rest not on human wisdom but on the power of God.

Towards the beginning of his letter, Paul stated that Christ had sent him to proclaim the gospel without resorting to eloquent wisdom so that the cross would not be emptied of its power (1:17). The good news needs no help to do its work from those to whom it has been entrusted, because it has its origin in God alone.

It was not as though Paul had never used human eloquence in his preaching. We see him in the book of Acts arguing with the Athenians on the Areopagus (Acts 17:16–34), but in Corinth he found himself with nothing to rely on except an invitation to trust in a crucified messiah. The art of rhetoric was highly prized in the ancient world, and those who could employ its tools were well placed to win arguments and carry off prizes. But in Corinth Paul chose to emphasise the paradox of a crucified Lord, for his hearers here needed to put their faith in the foolishness and weakness of God in order to come to know God's power to save.

This is the real mystery of the cross. It is what was so ridiculous in the eyes of the worldly wise and still appears so today. How can the failure and humiliation of crucifixion be the key to the meaning of life? Paul was convinced that this apparently foolish message contained within it the very power of God, at work by the Spirit in ways that humans cannot control or account for, other than ascribe it to God.

Take a cross or a picture of one and ponder its mystery for your life today.

LIZ HOARE

Thursday 31 July   **1 Corinthians 2:6–10 (NRSV)**

God's hidden wisdom revealed

Yet among the mature we do speak wisdom, though it is not a wisdom of this age or of the rulers of this age, who are being destroyed. But we speak God's wisdom, a hidden mystery, which God decreed before the ages for our glory and which none of the rulers of this age understood, for if they had, they would not have crucified the Lord of glory. But, as it is written, 'What no eye has seen, nor ear heard, nor the human heart conceived, what God has prepared for those who love him' – God has revealed to us through the Spirit, for the Spirit searches everything, even the depths of God.

Verse 8 is one of the most poignant verses of the Bible. If ever we need a more stark warning about the dangers of power and worldly wisdom, here it is. The Lord of glory, the one who created all things, the one in whom 'all the fullness of God was pleased to dwell' (Colossians 1:19), was subjected to the most cruel and humiliating death on a cross because those wielding power did not recognise him for who he was. The Corinthian Christians might well pause and reconsider their attitude to power and to what destructive ends it could lead.

Paul is not interested in worldly power or human wisdom, however, but rather the hidden wisdom that lies at the heart of God and how it is revealed. Just as each individual human can only truly know their own heart, so the Holy Spirit of God is the one who knows the deepest heart of God and makes God known. Now at last, Paul is saying, the hiddenness of God has been revealed in Jesus Christ, who is the embodiment of the true wisdom that comes from God alone. The great dividing line is between those who belong to the present age and those who, through faith in Christ, belong to the new age, the age to come. The importance of spiritual maturity is introduced here and will govern how Paul tackles the issues that have arisen in Corinth.

Ponder the difference it will make to you today to know that we have been given the Spirit of God.

LIZ HOARE

Friday 1 August — 1 Corinthians 3:1–4 (NRSV)

Not mature enough for solid food

And so, brothers and sisters, I could not speak to you as spiritual people but rather as fleshly, as infants in Christ. I fed you with milk, not solid food, for you were not yet ready for solid food. Even now you are still not ready, for you are still fleshly. For as long as there is jealousy and quarrelling among you, are you not fleshly and behaving according to human inclinations? For when one says, 'I belong to Paul', and another, 'I belong to Apollos', are you not all too human?

Weaning an infant on to their first solid food is a significant growth stage. It is a gradual process, and not always straightforward. All the same, it is vital that the baby starts to eat solid food if they are to grow out of babyhood into a fully mature human being. In addition it opens up a whole new world of taste and texture and culinary delights. To Paul's sorrow, the Corinthians are still behaving like infants and are therefore unable to receive the spiritual wisdom that is the mark of Christian maturity.

There is a sense in which we always remain beginners in the Christian life, needing to retain a child-like trust. But this does not preclude learning to plumb the riches of God in Christ. The depths of God that Paul has mentioned already are there for believers to discover through prayer and practice with the help of the Spirit.

In using the metaphor of milk and solid food, Paul is pointing out the irony that those who boasted of being wise and rich in spiritual things are in fact nothing of the sort. He suggests that, in fact, the jealousy and quarrelling reported to him is the behaviour of 'people of the flesh' (v. 1), that is, people who cannot receive the truths that are communicated by the Spirit.

It must have been hard for the Corinthians to hear the apostle's rebuke, especially as it comes some time after their initial conversion. It emphasises the importance of growing in the Christian life, along with a reminder of the pastoral implications of spiritual growth taking time and being sometimes uneven.

Lord, may your Spirit lead me into your wisdom. Amen.

LIZ HOARE

Saturday 2 August 1 Corinthians 3:5, 9–11 (NRSV)

God the master builder

What then is Apollos? What is Paul? Servants through whom you came to believe, as the Lord assigned to each… For we are God's coworkers, working together; you are God's field, God's building. According to the grace of God given to me, like a wise master builder I laid a foundation, and someone else is building on it. Let each builder choose with care how to build on it. For no one can lay any foundation other than the one that has been laid; that foundation is Jesus Christ.

In today's passage Paul takes up another metaphor to teach the Corinthians about the way God works through human beings to fulfil his purposes. Rather than play one evangelist off against another as the Corinthians were doing, Paul shows how in fact they all have a part to play and no one is more important than another, except for Christ himself. Christ is the only foundation for this kind of building, for it is about the kingdom of God.

Notice how Paul expresses himself through this imagery. He is not claiming superiority or suggesting his part is lacking because someone else is building on the foundation he laid. Although I know of people who have built their own house, most of them call on others to assist with particular skills – a bricklayer here, a plumber there – and it is uplifting when all work together as a team. Each person has to pull their weight and give of their best if the building is to be successful, and it would be no use if the bricklayer, for example, decided to ignore the foundations and add a wall or change the position of the doors and windows.

Paul has posed a question: 'What then is Apollos? What is Paul?' (v. 5). The factions at Corinth have been arguing about this very thing, but Paul is adamant that what counts is God, whose servants they both are. There is much here for the way we build God's church today. Do we idolise individual leaders or pit one big platform speaker against another? How much of a team are our congregations, however large or small? Most important of all, are we building on Jesus Christ as the only sure foundation?

Lord, we pray that your church will only ever seek to build on you as our one true foundation. Amen.

LIZ HOARE

Sunday 3 August   **1 Corinthians 4:8–10 (NRSV)**

Fatherly discipline

Already you have all you want! Already you have become rich! Quite apart from us you have become kings! If only you had become kings, so that we might be kings with you! For I think that God has exhibited us apostles as last of all, as though sentenced to death, because we have become a spectacle to the world, to angels and to humans. We are fools for the sake of Christ, but you are sensible people in Christ. We are weak, but you are strong. You are honoured, but we are dishonoured.

We can hear the sarcasm rippling through Paul's admonition at this point in his letter. He is following the pride and conceit of the Corinthian Christians to its logical conclusion. He has exhorted them to think of himself and his fellow apostles as servants of Christ and stewards of God's mysteries, not as a leader who is lording it over them. Here is a model for anyone called to minister to God's people in any circumstance.

As for his parody of their self-promotion, the irony is that they do have everything they need because of God's grace given in Christ. Yet they have been bewitched by worldly conceit, 'puffed up' like peacocks, thinking they are rich, wise, even kings. Not so, insists Paul. Whatever they have and are, they owe entirely to Christ and his grace. He contrasts them with the apostles: fools for Christ, weak and disreputable.

Imagine a platform speaker at a Christian event being advertised like this. Paul even likens the apostles to the condemned, who were brought out at the end of a display in the arena, sure to die either by the sword or by wild beasts. He is determined to get his point across, not to shame, but to discipline the immature Corinthians. Yet in comparing himself to spectacles in the arena, he is likening himself to Jesus.

Did the Corinthians get the point? We may imagine the anguish he feels at a distance, unable to speak to them face to face and deeply concerned for their spiritual maturity. His words may lead us to reflect on the riches we have received from God by grace alone.

Thank God for his grace, naming the gifts you are especially grateful for today.

LIZ HOARE

Monday 4 August   1 Corinthians 5:1–4a (NRSV)

Sexual scandal in the church

It is actually reported that there is sexual immorality among you and the sort of sexual immorality that is not found even among gentiles, for a man is living with his father's wife. And you are arrogant! Should you not rather have mourned, so that he who has done this would have been removed from among you? For I, though absent in body, am present in spirit, and as if present I have already pronounced judgement in the name of the Lord Jesus on the man who has done such a thing.

Today's portion of Paul's letter makes for sad reading, even though we know that the 21st-century church is so different from that of the first century. Why is this so? How could the gospel message that was preached to them have been so misinterpreted? It seems that freedom in Christ was seen to have no limits, even on moral behaviour. Had they become so spiritual that what they did with their bodies did not matter?

This is not the only instance of such reasoning among Christian believers, and as later parts of the letter show, it can have serious consequences, not only for those who act this out, but for others struggling with their consciences. What is more, it can ruin the witness of the church to outsiders. In this case, Paul exclaims that not even pagans would do such a thing. So where should the line of Christian freedom be drawn?

Paul has to deal not only with the issue itself, but also the Corinthians' arrogant attitude towards such behaviour. In this respect, the issue is further evidence of the Corinthians' pride. The way Paul deals with the issue gives rise to a further question for us today from these verses: how should discipline be imposed in the church? Paul does not hesitate to pronounce judgement, something we have become much more reticent about doing, but he is clear that harm is being done within the body of Christ. He goes on to describe it as being like yeast that works its way through the entire lump of dough, a sobering image that challenges us to consider carefully what freedom in Christ should look like in today's society.

Lord Jesus Christ, have mercy on us sinners. Amen.

LIZ HOARE

Tuesday 5 August   **1 Corinthians 6:1–3, 7 (NRSV)**

Lawsuits in the church

When any of you has a grievance against another, do you dare to take it to court before the unrighteous, instead of taking it before the saints? Do you not know that the saints will judge the world? And if the world is to be judged by you, are you incompetent to try trivial cases? Do you not know that we are to judge angels, to say nothing of ordinary matters?… In fact, to have lawsuits at all with one another is already a defeat for you. Why not rather be wronged? Why not rather be defrauded? But you yourselves wrong and defraud – and brothers and sisters at that.

When dealing with sexual immorality, Paul spoke of handing the offender 'over to Satan' (1 Corinthians 5:5), by which he meant the one who rules the sphere outside the church. Turning to lawsuits, he expresses his astonishment that the Corinthian Christians should take their grievances to judges who operated in another sphere rather than in the body of Christ. He sees the body of Christ (drawing on passages like Daniel 7) as the future judges of the entire world, indeed of the cosmos, since they will also be judging angels.

Corinth may have prided itself on being a Roman colony, and therefore subject to the imperial justice system of Rome, but Christians bow to a different Lord, the one in whom true justice is found. Paul is trying to help the Corinthians understand that they must no longer march to the drumbeat of the world, but should be seen to be different by the way they live.

Taking each other to secular courts to be judged by unrighteous judges is the antithesis of this. This is partly because the unrighteous judges have not been justified by Christ, but it also means, inevitably, that disputes will be played out in full view of a watching world that will not be impressed by claims that Christians are people who have been given a new identity in Christ and live differently as a consequence. It would of course be better by far not to fall out in the first place, but if disputes do arise, then they should seek someone to arbitrate from within the church community.

Here is another area of church life where we continue to struggle to be different.

Pray that we might begin by finding ways to heal differences between ourselves so that we shine as lights in a darkened world.

LIZ HOARE

Wednesday 6 August   **1 Corinthians 6:12–15a (NRSV)**

Glorify God in our bodies

'All things are permitted for me,' but not all things are beneficial. 'All things are permitted for me,' but I will not be dominated by anything. 'Food is meant for the stomach and the stomach for the food,' and God will destroy both one and the other. The body is meant not for sexual immorality but for the Lord and the Lord for the body. And God raised the Lord and will also raise us by his power. Do you not know that your bodies are members of Christ?

Bodies are a big issue in the 21st century. From weight to clothes, from re-inventing our image with the help of social media to idolising certain body images, we are body-obsessed.

How much do our bodies really matter? A great deal, says Paul, but not for the reasons we might think. The Corinthians were arguing that, having been set free from the law of sin that binds, they were no longer in its grip and could therefore do whatever felt good. Not so, says Paul, because you are members of Christ. How can we go on indulging in a lifestyle that contradicts his? Paul rightly points out that certain behaviours lead straight back into slavery to sin, and food and sex are two obvious examples.

Libertarian behaviour suggests that the body does not matter, but Paul never takes a dualist approach to body and spirit. Our bodies may die, but God, who raised Jesus, will also raise us in the same way. This sheds a whole new light on what we do with our physical bodies. They are not inconvenient matter that will be discarded, and they are most certainly affected by the way we treat them. This important principle will receive in-depth treatment towards the end of the letter, when Paul talks about the resurrection (1 Corinthians 15).

Learning to think in a Christian way about food and sex were two troublesome examples of navigating the new lifestyle that the church in Corinth had been given, and those issues dominate much of Paul's first letter. As with other topics in 1 Corinthians, they still resonate with how we seek to live for Christ today.

---

*Lord Jesus, help me to value and respect
the body you have given me. Amen.*

LIZ HOARE

Thursday 7 August   **1 Corinthians 7:1–3, 5 (NRSV)**

Marriage instructions

Now concerning the matters about which you wrote: 'It is good for a man not to touch a woman.' But because of cases of sexual immorality, each man should have his own wife and each woman her own husband. The husband should give to his wife what is due her and likewise the wife to her husband… Do not deprive one another except perhaps by agreement for a set time, to devote yourselves to prayer, and then come together again, so that Satan may not tempt you because of your lack of self-control.

It is immediately striking that Paul speaks to husbands and wives equally in this section. Marriage is a mutual arrangement and both parties matter equally. Paul is not a misogynist, and urges equality in the way husband and wife treat one another.

The other interesting point about this passage is that Paul is quoting a letter that has been sent to him seeking advice, and it provides a window into life within the Corinthian church. It seems that some were taking the opposite line from those who said that freedom in Christ meant doing whatever we like, and instead were promoting sexual abstinence as the way to spiritual holiness.

As with the other issues in Corinth, this attitude to sexuality has continued to affect and influence the church since early times, and it involves our attitude towards the physical. The body is not a hindrance to holiness, but part of our humanity. With regard to the married state, Paul is at ease with the idea of a period of abstinence from sexual relations for the purpose of prayer – we might think in terms of going on a retreat – but he is also clear that one's spouse is the only person with whom sexual relations are permissible.

Paul writes out of pastoral concern and offers advice that stems from reflecting on scripture and experience. He is firmly theological in his understanding of the place of the body in spirituality. We do not know whether Paul was ever married, but he respects both the celibate state and the married in his thinking.

Pray for married couples and also for singles in your church as they seek to follow Christ.

LIZ HOARE

Friday 8 August   **1 Corinthians 7:27, 29–31 (NRSV)**

Stay as you are

Are you bound to a wife? Do not seek to be free. Are you free from a wife? Do not seek a wife… I mean, brothers and sisters, the appointed time has grown short; from now on, let even those who have wives be as though they had none, and those who mourn as though they were not mourning, and those who rejoice as though they were not rejoicing, and those who buy as though they had no possessions, and those who deal with the world as though they had no dealings with it. For the present form of this world is passing away.

Chapter 7's overall message is to not try to change the status someone had when they converted. It is repeated three times, in verses 17, 20 and 24. This did not apply to their moral behaviour, though: if they were professional thieves, that had to change immediately. Yet with regard to marriage or social status, they should persevere in the same state as before.

Paul's words sound harsh, even unreasonable, but the principle that governed his thinking was the Christian's new status in Christ, against which everything else was secondary. In the light of this, his words continue to challenge us in our 'get ahead' society. What makes us restless and pulls us towards a glittering alternative life? A friend gets a promotion, the neighbours move to a bigger house in a better postcode, our best friend leaves his spouse for someone new? How do our desires sit with Christ's call on us? Paul helps us to take the long view and practise contentment. He likely had the Lord's return in mind when he wrote verse 31; he may also have been thinking of the severe famine that struck the empire around this time.

N.T. Wright translates verse 31 as 'The pattern of this world, you see, is passing away' and argues that Paul may be saying that the present crisis cannot last forever, so it is best not to make great changes for the moment. Interestingly, Ignatius of Loyola, founder of the Jesuits, also urged anyone in a state of turbulence – what he called 'desolation' – to not make changes.

Is there something you are thinking of doing that might benefit from waiting? Whatever situations we are in, the most important guiding principle is that we are faithful to the Lord Jesus.

Pray for the gift of spiritual discernment.

LIZ HOARE

Saturday 9 August   **1 Corinthians 8:1, 9–11 (NRSV)**

Food offered to idols

Now concerning food sacrificed to idols: we know that 'all of us possess knowledge'. Knowledge puffs up but love builds up… But take care that this liberty of yours does not somehow become a stumbling block to the weak. For if others see you, who possess knowledge, eating in the temple of an idol, might they not, since their conscience is weak, be encouraged to the point of eating food sacrificed to idols? So by your knowledge the weak brother or sister for whom Christ died is destroyed.

We are some way off Paul's great passage about love in 1 Corinthians 13, but these words prepare the ground in real issues and remind us that love is much, much more than a cosy feeling. In addressing the issue of food that has been offered to idols being sold in the marketplace, Paul is putting flesh on phrases such as 'Love is patient; love is kind… It does not insist on its own way… It bears all things' (1 Corinthians 13:4–7).

Paul is concerned both for those who are puffed up with a false kind of knowledge, for whom he desires a 'better way' (13:1) and also for those whose faith is being undermined by their apparent freedom. 'All things are permitted for me' (6:12), but it is not all about me anymore, now that I belong to Christ.

The knowledgeable members of the church think they are mature because they know that idols are just that – blocks of wood and stone with no life in them whatsoever and therefore food can't be contaminated by being offered in their temples. Paul, however, calls out their superior knowledge for the selfish thing it is. As members of the body of Christ, we do not live for ourselves anymore and we must be considerate of others who might be derailed in their faith by our 'freedom'. Paul uses strong language: such arrogant behaviour might destroy someone with a weaker conscience. In contrast with knowledge that puffs up, Paul's guiding principle for our actions is love that builds up.

How do my lifestyle choices undermine or build up other believers in my fellowship?

LIZ HOARE

Introduction

Bible chemicals

I have noted in a previous contribution to *New Daylight* that I began my working life as a chemistry master in a huge comprehensive school in Sunderland. I remember with affection the first week of each new academic year when classes of fresh-faced eleven-year-olds would come for their first chemistry lesson in my laboratory. There was a sense of awe and wonder as they had their first encounters with Bunsen burners and the like. Fifty years on in this digital age, I wonder if that still applies?

I would gather the children around my demonstration bench at the front of the lab and, after the obvious preliminaries, I would ask a question along the lines of 'Can any of you see any chemicals and can you name any chemicals?' Their eyes would drift towards the reagent bottles to either side of the blackboard, and reply, 'sulphuric acid', 'sodium hydroxide', 'copper sulphate'.

All these answers were, of course, 100% correct, but my aim in the lesson was to steer them towards the realisation that literally everything they could see around them – including me and their classmates – was made up of chemicals. The basic building blocks of our world are elements. There are over a hundred of them, but many are very rare and indeed some only exist in the laboratory. Amusingly for me, several 'new' elements have been discovered since my university days over 50 years ago. These 100+ elements can combine in an infinite number of ways to form compounds. Probably the simplest example, the elements hydrogen and oxygen combine to form the compound water.

Importantly in the context of this series, with the exception of modern manufactured compounds, such as plastics, these same elements and compounds existed all those thousands of years ago when the Bible was being written. Moreover, some of them are actually named or alluded to.

For the next two weeks, then, we will explore some of these. But, for those of you who shudder at the memory of chemistry lessons – do not worry. This is very gentle.

A little aside – the Latin name for lead always raised a few laughs with the eleven-year olds of the 1970s. It is *plumbum*.

GEOFFREY LOWSON

Sunday 10 August   **Genesis 1:1–5 (KJV)**

Beginning with 'water'

In the beginning God created the heaven and the earth. And the earth was without form, and void; and darkness was upon the face of the deep. And the Spirit of God moved upon the face of the waters. And God said, Let there be light: and there was light. And God saw the light, that it was good: and God divided the light from the darkness. And God called the light Day, and the darkness he called Night. And the evening and the morning were the first day.

These opening verses of the Bible are so familiar and indeed much loved, whether we think of the creation story as a lovely parable or regard it more literally. Whichever the case, it is beautiful literature.

But these verses are not without difficulty. Both the Jewish and Christian faiths embrace the doctrine of *ex nihilo* – creation out of nothing – and yet, reading Genesis 1 at face value, water already seems to be there. It just is.

On this occasion we must leave this dilemma to the scholars and philosophers, but it is worth noting three things. First there is the reference 'without form, and void' (v. 2). Indeed, water has no form but takes the form of its container. Second, we read of 'the deep', which is often used in association with the sea and carries with it a sense of disorder – almost a power set against God. Finally, we have the image of God's Spirit moving over the waters.

Water is so ordinary and so much part of our lives (in fact we are 60% water) that we could be forgiven for not thinking of it as a chemical, but of course it is. Furthermore, we all know that this chemical is one of the basics of all life and very precious – more precious than those of us in the western world perhaps appreciate. But 'it just is'!

Creator God, we thank you for the gift of water, this most basic of chemicals yet wondrous beyond words. For ourselves, we pray that we might use it wisely and treat it with respect. For others without it, we pray for governments and charities striving to bring the gift of clean, fresh water to all. Amen.

GEOFFREY LOWSON

Monday 11 August   Exodus 1:22—2:3 (NRSV)

Bitumen: the ancient world's mastic

Then Pharaoh commanded all his people, 'Every son that is born to the Hebrews you shall throw into the Nile, but you shall let every daughter live.' Now a man from the house of Levi went and married a Levite woman. The woman conceived and bore a son, and when she saw that he was a fine baby, she hid him for three months. When she could hide him no longer she got a papyrus basket for him and plastered it with bitumen and pitch; she put the child in it and placed it among the reeds on the bank of the river.

Bitumen is a naturally occurring chemical and, put very simply, it is the thickest form of crude oil. It is a black, extremely glutinous liquid, and it occurs naturally in various parts of the world. Significantly, in terms of our theme, there are large deposits near the Dead Sea.

The earliest known uses of bitumen take us back 40,000 years, when it was used as a glue to attach arrow heads to wooden shafts. In ancient Egypt it was used in the process of mummification. Yet in the context of today's passage of scripture, it is well-documented that it was used for the construction of buildings and water-proofing (caulking) of reed boats. In 2016, it was shown that the seventh-century ship buried at Sutton Hoo in Suffolk had been made water tight with bitumen from the Dead Sea.

With this background, the notion of the baby Moses' basket being covered in bitumen to make it watertight ties in with the practice of the time. (Pitch is basically the same substance.) In the ancient world, there were other stories very like this one, but perhaps what makes this different is the specific mention of the tribe of Levi. In the Hebrew language the root meaning of Levi involves attachment to or a special relationship with God. Consequently, as Levites, Moses' parents were, if you like, agents of God. God's purpose was being fulfilled through them.

Throughout history mothers have wanted to protect their children. Reflect upon the risk Moses' mother took and how she must have felt.

GEOFFREY LOWSON

Tuesday 12 August   **2 Kings 5:1, 10, 14 (NRSV, abridged)**

Sulphur: an ancient and modern medicine

Naaman, commander of the army of the king of Aram, was a great man and in high favour with his master… The man, though a mighty warrior, suffered from leprosy… Elisha sent a messenger to him, saying, 'Go, wash in the Jordan seven times, and your flesh shall be restored, and you shall be clean'… So he went down and immersed himself seven times in the Jordan, according to the word of the man of God; his flesh was restored like the flesh of a young boy, and he was clean.

Tucked on a shelf in the understair cupboard we have a bottle of sulphur shampoo; it is for our dog Bess if she gets an itchy skin. People with skin problems are sometimes prescribed ointments which contain sulphur compounds, and indeed you may have heard of a group of medicines known as sulphanilamides.

Naaman's leprosy? It is widely acknowledged by biblical scholars that in the Bible the term 'leprosy', while sometimes referring to the specific illness of Hansen's disease, is also used to describe other skin conditions. Given his position and place in society, it is almost impossible to conceive of Naaman having what we now call leprosy. Perhaps he had severe psoriasis or eczema.

I have always loved this story of Naaman, who rather reluctantly bathed in the River Jordan until his skin condition was cured. The Jordan, in fact, does have some natural sulphur springs on its banks, so this may well have been the cause of the cure; furthermore, the number seven represents completeness and so Naaman bathed until the treatment was complete.

You may know of a sulphur spring near you – there is usually a smell like rotten eggs. ('Brimstone' in the Bible refers to burning sulphur.)

The story of Naaman features some unnamed characters, but in fact they are key to the outcome. There is the servant girl who directed Naaman to Elisha, and there are Naaman's own servants who persuaded him to do as Elisha had asked and bathe in the Jordan.

We thank you, Lord, for those people in our own lives, including many 'unnamed characters', who have supported us, guided us and influenced us for good in our journey through life.

GEOFFREY LOWSON

Wednesday 13 August   **Ezekiel 16:3–5a (NRSV)**

Sodium chloride: the ancient world's exfoliant?

Thus says the Lord God to Jerusalem: Your origin and your birth were in the land of the Canaanites; your father was an Amorite and your mother a Hittite. As for your birth, on the day you were born your navel cord was not cut, nor were you washed with water to cleanse you, nor rubbed with salt, nor wrapped in cloths. No eye pitied you to do any of these things for you out of compassion for you…

Sodium chloride is salt; many people put it on their fish and chips and other foods. It is mentioned six times in the New Testament but 40 in the Old Testament. No wonder, for it was one of the basics of everyday life in the ancient world, being used for preserving and flavouring food, in the production of leather, for cleansing, and in ritual offerings. It was so important as a trading commodity that at times it was as precious as gold and wars were fought over it.

These opening verses of Ezekiel 16 are harsh, and the chapter continues in the same vein. In contemporary parlance we might say that the prophet is having a rant about Israel's behaviour, particularly in ignoring what God required of them. Yet, regrettably in Ezekiel's mind, God seemed not to punish Israel! Ezekiel felt that what was needed was some cleansing, because that had not happened at the very beginning – at Israel's birth.

This brings us to today's passage which mentions our chemical salt. Verse 4 describes exactly what happened at the birth of a child: the umbilical cord was cut, the baby was washed, and then the baby had salt rubbed into its skin, with particular attention paid to the neck, armpits, feet, hands and genitals. Salt was thought of as a disinfectant and what today we would call a skin conditioner. Additionally, it was thought that the salt protected from evil spirits and demons.

Interestingly this practice is maintained today among some Middle Eastern communities, particularly in Turkey, where babies are 'salted' anytime up to 40 days after birth.

'Salt is born of the purest parents: the sun and the sea' (Pythagoras).

GEOFFREY LOWSON

Thursday 14 August   **Mark 9:49—10:1 (NRSV)**

Salt again: in ritual

'For everyone will be salted with fire. Salt is good; but if salt has lost its saltiness, how can you season it? Have salt in yourselves, and be at peace with one another.' He left that place and went to the region of Judea and beyond the Jordan. And crowds again gathered around him, and, as was his custom, he again taught them.

Salt was so important in the lives of the people of the ancient world. It was, of course, used to preserve and to flavour, but it was also used ritually, as seen, for example, in Ezekiel 43:24: 'You shall present [the sacrificial animals] before the Lord, and the priests shall throw salt on them and offer them up as a burnt offering to the Lord.'

There are also several references to salt being a symbol of enduring agreements; the term used is 'a covenant of salt'. This could refer to a covenant between people and God, between two individuals or between groups of people. The house of David is, for example, said to have received the kingdom by a 'covenant of salt' (2 Chronicles 13:5). And then there was the matter of relationships. When people ate together, they inevitably shared salt and the eating together fostered friendship. Even today there are Arabic expressions 'There is salt between us' and 'He has eaten of my salt'.

We can go a step further in our analysis. Because salt is both a preservative and an extremely stable chemical, the implication is that formal covenants and relationships made through salt would be stable and long lasting.

Today's passage of scripture appears in Matthew, Mark and Luke, slightly differently in each. It is a bit obscure, particularly because in reality salt never does lose its taste! However, it makes more sense in light of the 'covenant of salt'. At this point Jesus was teaching his disciples and reminding them of their sense of togetherness – of the covenant between them based upon their being together and sharing salt together. They would be successful only if they build upon that.

Next time you are having a meal with friends and you want to add salt, consider that you are cementing 'a covenant of salt'.

Give thanks for friendship and relationships
that are stable and long lasting.

GEOFFREY LOWSON

Friday 15 August   **Matthew 23:27–28 (REB)**

Whitewash: an ancient 'paint' which is still used

Alas for you, scribes and Pharisees, hypocrites! You are like tombs covered with whitewash; they look fine on the outside, but inside they are full of dead men's bones and of corruption. So it is with you; outwardly you look like honest men, but inside you are full of hypocrisy and lawlessness.

I live in a beautiful valley called Teesdale in the north-east of England. One distinctive feature is that most of the farm buildings on the north side of the river stand out, because they are 'painted' white; they all belong to the local estate. In truth the buildings are not painted, but whitewashed. I imagine that more senior readers will recall that before emulsion paint was the norm, many a ceiling and pantry was whitewashed.

If you heat limestone (calcium carbonate) to a high temperature, carbon dioxide is driven off and you are left with lime (calcium oxide). Stir water into the lime and you get a milky suspension known as slaked lime, which is basically whitewash. The clever twist, however, is that when painted on a wall, the whitewash reacts with the carbon dioxide in the atmosphere to turn back into calcium carbonate, giving a hard, protective 'paint'.

In Palestine it was normal to have tombs by the roadside, but this created a potential problem in that if someone were to touch a tomb, that person became ritually unclean. At the time of the Passover, the roads leading to Jerusalem became particularly busy and the chance of a pilgrim accidentally touching a tomb became very real. If they did, they would be prevented from sharing in the rituals of the festival. It was therefore Jewish practice in the previous month of Adar (March) to whitewash the tombs to make them very obvious. They looked clean and fresh and 'beautiful', but everyone knew what was inside.

Jesus' point is clear as he uses the analogy with reference to the scribes and Pharisees; they liked to give the outward impression of being virtuous but their inner lives told a different story.

'God has given you one face, and you make yourself another' (Hamlet, III.1).

GEOFFREY LOWSON

Saturday 16 August — **Malachi 3:1–2 (KJV)**

Caustic soda: treat with care

Behold, I will send my messenger, and he shall prepare the way before me: and the Lord, whom ye seek, shall suddenly come to his temple, even the messenger of the covenant, whom ye delight in: behold, he shall come, saith the Lord of hosts. But who may abide the day of his coming? and who shall stand when he appeareth? for he is like a refiner's fire, and like fullers' soap.

In one of the famous arias from Handel's *Messiah*, the expected Messiah is likened to 'a refiner's fire'. Handel does not, however, go on to mention 'fullers' soap'! This is today's chemical, which the Bible also refers to as lye.

Its chemical name is sodium hydroxide, which we sometimes call caustic soda; you may even have some in the house to clean your drains. In Palestine it was made by burning a plant called saltwort, which grows in abundance by the Dead Sea. If you add water to the resultant ash and allow them to react, you get a solution of sodium hydroxide.

'Fulling' or 'fullering' was the process of washing, bleaching and thickening of fibres or cloth prior to dyeing. The process was complex but in summary the cloth was soaked in cold water and then boiled in a solution of fullers' soap; it was then beaten and rinsed in flowing water, wrung out and put out in the sun to dry. The procedure produced a foul smell, so the whole process took place in a field well outside the city; indeed, there is a reference in Isaiah 7:3: 'Then the Lord said to Isaiah, "Go out to meet Ahaz… at the end of the conduit of the upper pool on the highway to the fuller's field"' (NRSV).

The passage today starts with good news for the people of Israel: God is coming! But then the reality – a reality which the people had forgotten. An element of God's coming involves judgement and purification. As the metallurgist's fire burns off the impurities, so the soap purges the dirt. We will return to this theme of purification again in these reflections.

How do you equate our image of a gentle, loving God with the judgemental God?

GEOFFREY LOWSON

Sunday 17 August   **John 18:16–18 (NRSV)**

Charcoal: a form of carbon

Peter was standing outside at the gate. So the other disciple, who was known to the high priest, went out, spoke to the woman who guarded the gate, and brought Peter in. The woman said to Peter, 'You are not also one of this man's disciples, are you?' He said, 'I am not.' Now the slaves and the police had made a charcoal fire because it was cold, and they were standing round it and warming themselves. Peter also was standing with them and warming himself.

There is something very human in this image of Peter and others standing around a fire. It takes me back to my childhood when I would help my father with a bonfire, or later, when my boys would help me. Bonfires are rather frowned upon these days, but they do seem to stir up something from deep within as one watches the flames and the glowing embers. There is something calming about them.

Jesus had been arrested and taken to the house of Annas the high priest, and Peter and the other disciple had gone with him. Here we have one of those heart-breaking encounters when Peter denied Jesus. But set alongside it we have this picture of Peter and the others standing around the charcoal fire. The situation must have been very tense and so perhaps watching the fire was more than just warming – perhaps it was also calming.

Pure carbon occurs naturally in two forms, diamond and graphite, the latter being the stuff of pencil lead. Another pure form is charcoal, beloved by men with barbeques! Charcoal is produced by heating wood in the absence of air; wood is about 50 per cent carbon and in the heating process the other chemicals are driven off, leaving just the carbon. Wood charcoal production goes right back into ancient history; it was a necessary fuel both domestically and for refining metals.

I wonder if Peter recalled the courtyard when, sometime later, he was the one who brought ashore the fish to cook on the charcoal fire with the risen Jesus. I wonder if that was a healing experience.

Pray for countries, such as Malawi and Somalia, where charcoal production is an important source of income, but is leading to deforestation.

GEOFFREY LOWSON

Monday 18 August   **Jeremiah 2:20–22 (KJV)**

Nitre: a bit of a riddle

For of old time I have broken thy yoke, and burst thy bands; and thou saidst, I will not transgress; when upon every high hill and under every green tree thou wanderest, playing the harlot. Yet I had planted thee a noble vine, wholly a right seed: how then art thou turned into the degenerate plant of a strange vine unto me? For though thou wash thee with nitre, and take thee much soap, yet thine iniquity is marked before me, saith the Lord God.

My father was born in 1902 and at the age of nine became ill with a burst appendix. The only transport to the hospital 25 miles away was in a horse and trap, and to make it worse the horse had to have a rest on the way. He would relish telling this tale to remind people that not everything about 'the good old days' was good!

We all look back through rose-tinted spectacles from time to time, and so does Jeremiah. In today's passage he is railing against the people for deviating from the true worship of God, but he begins the chapter by saying, 'I remember the devotion of your youth, your love as a bride, how you followed me in the wilderness' (Jeremiah 2:2, NRSV). The truth is they were certainly not perfect in the wilderness either. But Jeremiah is angry and says that no amount of washing can take away their sin.

Today's chemical could slip under the radar unless we look in the King James Version. It is nitre, but contemporary translations use more generic names, such as soda, for good reason, it would seem. Nitre is potassium nitrate, also known as saltpetre, but there are no deposits of that in Israel. There are, however, huge deposits of sodium carbonate near Sodom in southern Israel, and that chemical was known as 'nitron'. Furthermore, whereas the latter could be used for washing (indeed it is sometimes referred to as washing soda), potassium nitrate certainly would not be!

Nitre or nitron? Dare I say it, perhaps the composers of the Authorised Version got a little confused.

Give thanks and pray for those who translate and interpret the Bible.

GEOFFREY LOWSON

Tuesday 19 August   **Deuteronomy 8:7–9 (NRSV)**

Copper and King Solomon

For the Lord your God is bringing you into a good land, a land with flowing streams, with springs and underground waters welling up in valleys and hills, a land of wheat and barley, of vines and fig trees and pomegranates, a land of olive oil and honey, a land where you may eat bread without scarcity, where you will lack nothing, a land whose stones are iron and from whose hills you may mine copper.

I am not sure how popular the novel *King Solomon's Mines* is these days – probably a bit 'old hat'. However, it seems that the mines did exist, although not as envisioned by Rider Haggard back in 1885. And they were not gold mines.

Six metal elements are mentioned in the Bible: gold, silver, lead, tin, copper and iron. Additionally, there are many references to bronze, an alloy of copper and tin. But none of these were mined in ancient Israel, not even the copper and iron that Moses promised.

What then of King Solomon's mines? Biblical scholars have long debated how Solomon, who reigned over Israel from 970 to 930BC, amassed his fortune. In the 1930s, Nelson Glueck, an American archaeologist, suggested that the legendary mines were in fact the Timna copper mines that had existed in what is now the very south of modern-day Israel, just north of the port resort of Eliat. Glueck's theory could not be verified, because the ruins of the mines could not be dated to Solomon's reign. However, in 2013 Israeli archaeologists accurately carbon-dated organic remains from the Timna Valley ruins to 930BC, the end of the great king's reign. Most biblical scholars now agree that copper from these mines was indeed the source of Solomon's wealth.

If one is allowed to have favourite passages of scripture, Deuteronomy 8 is one of mine. It evokes childhood memories of Harvest Thanksgiving services and of many a sermon preached as life went on. It is so full of optimism, promise and hope; after everything the people had gone through in the wilderness this is what they could look forward to.

'You are never too old to set another goal or to dream a new dream'
(C.S. Lewis, 1898–1963).

GEOFFREY LOWSON

Wednesday 20 August   **Mark 2:21–22 (NRSV)**

Ethanol: the alcoholic chemical in wine

'No one sews a piece of unshrunk cloth on an old cloak; otherwise, the patch pulls away from it, the new from the old, and a worse tear is made. Similarly, no one puts new wine into old wineskins; otherwise, the wine will burst the skins, and the wine is lost, and so are the skins, but one puts new wine into fresh wineskins.'

Years ago, I helped in a prison chaplaincy. One evening there was a kerfuffle because an inmate was thought to have some alcohol hidden away. It transpired that he had bought some apple juice from the prison shop, taken some grapes from the canteen, peeled them, popped the skin in the juice and because the bloom on the skin has traces of yeast – 'Hey presto', some very basic wine, the alcoholic constituent of which is a chemical called ethanol.

Throughout history, humankind has had a relationship with wine; indeed it was very much part of life in the ancient world. Water was the basic liquid for cooking, but it was not advisable to drink it; there was milk from goats and sheep and juice from fruits, but a staple drink was wine.

The wine was produced from grape juice and after the fermentation process was complete, it was stored in jars and sealed with a layer of olive oil to stop it oxidising and turning sour. For everyday use it was transferred to wineskins.

Jesus' message to his listeners in the parable was straightforward enough. He was bringing something quite new into the world and he was announcing that God was going to work through him in a new way – a way that could not be constrained by old ideas.

New wineskins had a certain elasticity, whereas old skins became brittle. Jesus was asking for an elasticity in his listeners' minds, so that they could accept new truths and contemplate new ways.

By the way, the prisoner kept his 'wine' in the tubular leg of his chair. How is that for elasticity of thinking?

Lord, open my heart and mind to new thoughts and ideas,
so that I may see you more clearly, love you more dearly
and follow you more nearly, day by day. Amen.

GEOFFREY LOWSON

Thursday 21 August **Matthew 27:33–35 (KJV)**

Acetic acid: we put it on our chips (with salt)

And when they were come unto a place called Golgotha, that is to say, a place of a skull, they gave him vinegar to drink mingled with gall: and when he had tasted thereof, he would not drink. And they crucified him, and parted his garments, casting lots: that it might be fulfilled which was spoken by the prophet, They parted my garments among them, and upon my vesture did they cast lots.

Yesterday we noted that wine left exposed to air turns sour. Chemically speaking, the ethanol reacts with the oxygen in the air to form a solution of acetic acid, which can be called vinegar. In fact the word derives from the French *vinaigre*, meaning sour wine. Most modern translations use 'sour wine' rather than 'vinegar', but for me the latter creates what I would describe as a shudder factor rather more vividly.

Like wine, vinegar is as old as civilization itself: traces of it have been found in Egyptian urns from around 3000BC, and Babylonian scrolls recording the use of vinegar date even earlier, to around 5000BC. It was used both to flavour food and to preserve it and was also used in some folk medicines. Interestingly, my grandmother's remedy for a tickly cough was a mixture of butter, sugar and vinegar, administered on a spoon. As I recall, it worked!

The phrase 'and they crucified him' is so brief and matter of fact that it belies the full horror of the event. It was so horrible in fact that it was the accepted custom for the women of Jerusalem to give any condemned person a drugged drink to dull their senses. This offering was based upon both human compassion and an adherence to an instruction in Proverbs 31:6, which reads: 'Give strong drink to one who is perishing.'

Matthew suggests that the drug was gall, an extract from the wormwood plant, but in the parallel passage, Mark refers to myrrh. Other historical documents suggest frankincense. The significant thing to note, perhaps, is that Jesus refused the drugged drink in order to endure his suffering to the end.

Vinegar makes one shudder! The suffering of others makes one shudder.

Lord, ease the burden of all those who have to suffer this day. Amen.

GEOFFREY LOWSON

Friday 22 August   **Amos 7:7–9a (NRSV)**

Lead: *plumbum* again

This is what he showed me: the Lord was standing beside a wall built with a plumb line, with a plumb line in his hand. And the Lord said to me, 'Amos, what do you see?' And I said, 'A plumb line.' Then the Lord said, 'See, I am setting a plumb line in the midst of my people Israel; I will spare them no longer; the high places of Isaac shall be made desolate, and the sanctuaries of Israel shall be laid waste.'

The metal lead has been used in ancient civilizations for 9,000 years. It is mentioned by name nine times in scripture, but there are other 'hidden' references. The pigment vermilion, which is a lead compound, is mentioned three times; there are references to eye make-up, which was a lead ore called galena, and of course the plumb line noted above – a length of string with a piece of lead attached to it to determine the vertical.

The prophet Amos was 'a herdsman and dresser of sycamore [fig] trees' (Amos 7:14) based in a village near Bethlehem. He lived about 770BC, a period of relative peace and prosperity in the Hebrew kingdoms, but the negative aspect of all this was a life of excess for the rich, exploitation of the poor, loose moral standards, corruption in public life and religious observance based upon ritual rather than real faith. It was against all this that Amos felt called to preach.

Chapter seven contains a series of visions, of which today's passage is one. The whole point of a plumb line is that it cannot be anything but straight and vertical; it is an unchanging standard. Amos therefore uses it as symbol of a 'standard' – of God's standards.

There is an ominous turn here in that Amos seems to have lost hope for a turning back of the people towards God; rather, all will be destroyed. It is a rather depressing note, but we can take hope. Amos' emphasis upon justice – upon there being a standard, a plumb line – has inspired Christians the world over.

There are so many injustices in our modern world – Amos would have much to rail against! Identify one that is in the news and pray about it today.

GEOFFREY LOWSON

Saturday 23 August   **John 7:37–39 (NRSV)**

Finishing with water

On the last day of the festival, the great day, while Jesus was standing there, he cried out, 'Let anyone who is thirsty come to me, and let the one who believes in me drink. As the scripture has said, "Out of the believer's heart shall flow rivers of living water."' Now he said this about the Spirit, which believers in him were to receive; for as yet there was no Spirit, because Jesus was not yet glorified.

Two weeks ago we began in Genesis with the Spirit of God moving over the face of the water. Water crops up time and time again throughout the Bible, sometimes used straightforwardly but often taking on highly symbolic meaning. In Revelation we have the image of 'the river of the water of life, bright as crystal, flowing from the throne of God and of the Lamb' (Revelation 22:1). In worship, water is used symbolically and sacramentally; spiritual writers utilise it – St Francis wrote, 'Sister water, who is useful and humble, precious and pure.'

The festival referred to in our passage is the Festival of the Tabernacles, when the people made shelters from branches to remind them of their 40 years in the wilderness. A specific ritual, enacted to give thanks for water springing from the rock, involved drawing water from the Pool of Siloam and carrying it through the Water Gate into the temple. It is against this vivid background that Jesus spoke about a new thing, that is this life-giving Spirit which, unlike the water which has to be sought after and carried, is with us in abundance.

Scholars comment that this passage is difficult to translate; it could be the water of life pouring out of Jesus or alternatively, pouring out of us, that is 'the believer'. Well, if it can be either, perhaps it can be both! Surely part of our Christian life is to receive the gift and then to pour it out to others.

Each time you have a drink today, jot down those gifts that you feel have been 'poured' into you. Then in the days to come, reflect upon how you could use them for the good of others and for the furtherance of the kingdom.

GEOFFREY LOWSON

Introduction

Barnabas

We know surprisingly little about Barnabas. Luke's selective summary of early church history, Acts, introduces him in chapter 4; he then features in Acts 9—15, after which he is absent from the narrative. Paul refers briefly to him in 1 Corinthians 9 and in Galatians and Colossians; the latter two feed into our readings this week alongside passages from Acts.

In factual terms, his name was really Joseph; he was a Levite but had been living on Cyprus rather than in Judea; he was a relative of John Mark, also named in Acts and several epistles; and he was a travelling companion of Paul on the latter's earliest mission travels.

Yet this little-known man makes a big impression in several ways. To begin with, the name by which we know him was a nickname reflecting the way he encouraged people: note how often he does that in our readings. Watch also for the times when he is prepared to take risks, doing things which more cautious people might have hesitated to try, and how with hindsight these ventures prove significant later, even if not at once. It is also worth considering what roles Barnabas played in the teams among whom he served, and how those may have evolved over time.

You may want to notice in particular Barnabas' impact on two other men named above: John Mark and Paul. A tradition dating back to the second century names Mark as the author of the second of the biblical gospels, which scholars generally agree was the earliest to be written. Paul's writings are well known and the New Testament includes more than a dozen letters bearing his name. If, as the passages in Acts imply, Barnabas was at times a mentor to each of these significant figures, then it may be that we are indirectly indebted to him for around a third of the New Testament – which is no small sphere of influence!

As we look at some snapshots of incidents from Barnabas' life, you may need to dig a little to build a mental portrait of his character. My assessment would feature warmth, thoughtfulness, generosity, humility and courage. Perhaps you could ask yourself over the next eight days: what are Barnabas' most notable qualities?

MARTIN LECKEBUSCH

Sunday 24 August   **Acts 4:34–5:5 (TNIV, abridged)**

True or false?

From time to time those who owned land or houses sold them, brought the money… and put it at the apostles' feet, and it was distributed to anyone who had need. Joseph, a Levite from Cyprus, whom the apostles called Barnabas… sold a field he owned and brought the money… Now a man named Ananias, together with his wife Sapphira, also sold a piece of property. With his wife's full knowledge, he kept back part of the money for himself, but brought the rest… Then Peter said, 'Ananias, how is it that Satan has so filled your heart that you have lied to the Holy Spirit and have kept for yourself some of the money you received…? Didn't it belong to you before it was sold?… Wasn't the money at your disposal?' When Ananias heard this, he fell down and died.

Ananias and Sapphira both died suddenly after receiving a sharp rebuke from Peter. The sobering account of their demise comes remarkably soon after the Holy Spirit was poured out at Pentecost. At a time when many of Christ's followers were gladly making their resources available for others' benefit, these two pretended to be more generous than they were. Peter's reprimand is clear: they were under no compulsion to make any such donation at all. It seems that a desire to appear 'spiritual' overcame them, with disastrous consequences.

Clearly they are not the only people ever to have used dishonesty or pretence to retain their wealth or bolster their reputation. Maybe we ourselves have acted similarly. Few, if any, have faced Ananias' and Sapphira's fate, yet the Lord is still looking for holy integrity.

It is in this context that Luke introduces Barnabas, who had also made a property sale and a gift; in his case, however, it was done honestly and without fanfare. Perhaps this was part of a wider pattern of behaviour, leading to him being given a nickname which stuck: 'Barnabas' means 'son of encouragement'. Luke presents Barnabas as a godly contrast to Ananias and his wife, setting the scene for his significant involvement later in the church's story.

Help me, Lord Jesus, to live with true integrity and to be genuinely open-handed with my resources, of whatever kind they are. Amen.

MARTIN LECKEBUSCH

Monday 25 August   Acts 9:19–21, 26–28 (TNIV, abridged)

A friend indeed

Saul spent several days with the disciples in Damascus. At once he began to preach in the synagogues that Jesus is the Son of God. All those who heard him were astonished and asked, 'Isn't he the man who caused havoc in Jerusalem among those who call on this name? And hasn't he come here to take them as prisoners to the chief priests?'… When he came to Jerusalem, he tried to join the disciples, but they were all afraid of him, not believing that he really was a disciple. But Barnabas took him and brought him to the apostles. He told them how Saul on his journey had seen the Lord and that the Lord had spoken to him, and how in Damascus he had preached fearlessly in the name of Jesus. So Saul stayed with them… speaking boldly in the name of the Lord.

The conversion of Saul of Tarsus was one of the pivotal moments in the history of the early church – and the church very nearly squandered it. First in Damascus, then in Jerusalem, Saul's utter change of outlook caused consternation to the point of disbelief. He could so easily have been permanently ostracised by fearful and suspicious believers, leading to either frustrated inertia for Saul or a church split between those who trusted him and those who did not.

It took someone warm-hearted and open-minded to handle this situation; that was Barnabas. He clearly listened to the story Saul told and looked at the evidence carefully. This enabled him to become a truthful advocate for his new friend, as he courageously arranged for Saul to meet the apostles.

It was a risky move. What if Saul actually had been faking his conversion? What if Barnabas found himself rejected by the apostles as well? Yet he accepted the reality of Saul's encounter on the Damascus road, and the power of Saul's preaching evidently convinced him that this man had a genuine faith and showed great promise. Therefore, Barnabas was prepared to take that risk.

Father, is there someone near me who needs a friend to listen to their story, to stand up for them and to invest in their potential? Help me to know when and how to be the kind of person who does that. Amen.

MARTIN LECKEBUSCH

Tuesday 26 August — Acts 11:19–20, 22–26 (NIV, abridged)

A wise choice, a bold move

Those who had been scattered by the persecution that broke out when Stephen was killed travelled as far as Phoenicia, Cyprus and Antioch, spreading the word only among Jews. Some of them, however... began to speak to Greeks also... News of this reached the church in Jerusalem, and they sent Barnabas to Antioch. When he arrived and saw the evidence of the grace of God, he was glad and encouraged them all to remain true to the Lord. He was a good man, full of the Holy Spirit and faith, and a great number of people were brought to the Lord. Then Barnabas went to Tarsus to look for Saul, and when he found him, he brought him to Antioch. So for a whole year Barnabas and Saul met with the church and taught great numbers of people.

Barnabas' varied gifts again prove useful. This early in the story of the church's mission, telling the gospel to people with no Jewish heritage was unusual and potentially controversial. The church leaders in Jerusalem were either unsettled by what they heard from Antioch or at least concerned that Gentile converts in such a huge, cosmopolitan city should be properly established in the faith.

Choosing Barnabas to assess the situation was wise. His strong faith and godly character, coupled with roots outside Judea, made him eminently suitable. He approached the situation in Antioch with an open mind and heart, which made him able to discern God's hand in the developments there. He then proved able to encourage these new believers in their faith, rather than embroil them in difficult contemporary questions, such as those around circumcision and adherence to traditional food laws.

And once again, Barnabas took risks. The people who brought the gospel to Antioch had fled a persecution in which Saul had eagerly participated. Deliberately seeking him out to help teach Antioch's believers could have appeared insensitive. Yet Barnabas may already have known of Saul's call to preach to the Gentiles; the growth in the church (spiritually and probably numerically, too) certainly validated Barnabas' decision.

Lord, help me to use faith, discernment, encouragement and whatever other gifts you entrust to me to extend and build your church. Amen.

MARTIN LECKEBUSCH

Wednesday 27 August Galatians 2:11–14, 16 (TNIV, abridged)

Oops… even Barnabas!

When Cephas came to Antioch, I opposed him to his face, because he stood condemned. For before certain people came from James, he used to eat with the Gentiles. But when they arrived, he began to draw back and separate himself from the Gentiles because he was afraid of those who belonged to the circumcision group. The other Jews joined him in his hypocrisy… even Barnabas was led astray. When I saw that they were not acting in line with the truth of the gospel, I said to Cephas in front of them all, 'You are a Jew, yet you live like a Gentile and not like a Jew. How is it, then, that you force Gentiles to follow Jewish customs?… A person is not justified by observing the law, but by faith in Jesus Christ.'

It is impossible to date precisely the events recounted here, but Paul still finds it necessary, possibly some years after they occurred, to set the record straight. A public confrontation between two influential church leaders would inevitably have generated plenty of surprise, confusion – and even gossip. Garbled accounts of what happened were apparently still hindering Paul's effectiveness in Christ's service.

Questions over Old Testament circumcision rules and Jewish traditions around sharing meals with Gentiles touched many raw nerves among those early Christians, becoming hot topics when different ethnic and religious backgrounds collided. Paul saw the key principle clearly: faith in Christ superseded the old regulations. When Peter (Cephas) and others compromised on this, they had to be challenged. Peter was doubtless not intending to upset his Gentile friends. Nevertheless, his craven actions effectively endorsed traditional prejudices in a way that undermined the freedom announced in the gospel; that was what made his actions dangerously misleading.

Paul was incensed by Peter's hypocrisy and its impact on Gentile Christians – even more because of who else was involved. He expected better of Barnabas, a friend he respected and trusted, and consequently he was astonished that Barnabas, too, was implicated. Yet no leader is fully immune to failure.

Pray that we will put our leaders neither apparently above correction nor beyond the hope of restoration if at some point they do stumble.

MARTIN LECKEBUSCH

Thursday 28 August   **Acts 13:2–12 (NIV, abridged)**

Led by the Spirit

The Holy Spirit said, 'Set apart for me Barnabas and Saul for the work to which I have called them.' So after they had fasted and prayed, they placed their hands on them and sent them off. The two of them, sent on their way by the Holy Spirit… sailed… to Cyprus [and] proclaimed the word of God in the Jewish synagogues… They travelled through the whole island… They met a Jewish sorcerer… an attendant of the proconsul, Sergius Paulus. The proconsul… wanted to hear the word of God. But Elymas the sorcerer… opposed them… Saul… filled with the Holy Spirit, looked straight at Elymas and said, 'You are a child of the devil…' Immediately mist and darkness came over him… When the proconsul saw what had happened, he believed…

The church in Antioch came to play an important role in the spread of the gospel: it was from here that Saul's (Paul's) lengthy missionary travels began. Luke's account emphasises the Holy Spirit's role in these.

First, in Antioch, Luke shows the Spirit's call to individuals, confirmed through the whole church leadership during a time of dedicated worship which included fasting. Responding to this call was a major commitment for Barnabas and Paul, but it also cost that congregation two key leaders.

Cyprus could have been merely an obvious destination, given Barnabas' roots there, but the travellers were sensitive to the Spirit's leading. As they travelled, they preached first in the synagogues before turning to Gentile audiences. This became a strategy Paul followed for many years afterwards.

The Spirit was active again when, at Paphos, they faced spiritual opposition from a Jewish false prophet and sorcerer (v. 6). Paul's prophetic rebuke exposed this man's deceitful motivation (v. 10) and announced the Lord's hand was against him (v. 11); the apostle's warning was fulfilled when the sorcerer temporarily became unable to see. As a result the proconsul responded with faith to the gospel, which he had wanted to hear but had previously been unable to fully grasp. Whether the sorcerer repented is not recorded.

Holy Spirit, help me to be open to all your guidance,
by whatever means it comes. Amen.

MARTIN LECKEBUSCH

Friday 29 August   **Acts 13:1, 13–16, 42 (NIV, abridged)**

Second fiddle?

In the church at Antioch there were prophets and teachers: Barnabas… and Saul… From Paphos, Paul and his companions sailed to Perga in Pamphylia… From Perga they went on to Pisidian Antioch. On the Sabbath they entered the synagogue and sat down. After the reading from the Law and the Prophets, the leaders of the synagogue sent word to them, saying, 'Brothers, if you have a word of exhortation for the people, please speak.' Standing up, Paul motioned with his hand and said: 'Fellow Israelites and you Gentiles who worship God, listen to me!'… As Paul and Barnabas were leaving the synagogue, the people invited them to speak further about these things on the next Sabbath.

When Luke names the church leaders in Antioch, Barnabas is listed first and Paul (Saul) last, perhaps signifying that Barnabas was the most senior among the group, with Paul as the relative newcomer, still finding his feet. However, by the time they return from Cyprus to Asia Minor, Paul is taking a much more prominent role.

At the synagogue in another place named Antioch (the one in the province of Galatia), Paul is evidently the main speaker. Luke records a tour de force of a sermon, in which Paul recaps the broad sweep of his people's history from Moses and the Exodus to David, then John the Baptist and Jesus. He shows how Jesus fulfils God's promises from past ages before calling on his hearers to believe in Jesus and receive forgiveness.

How might Barnabas have felt about the way their mission was going? Paul was, after all, someone whose Christian service Barnabas had nurtured, becoming an advocate for Paul when many people were suspicious of his credentials. Yet now Barnabas was rather overshadowed by someone he had mentored. Did he find that difficult or was he content to step into the background as Paul's preaching became consistently powerful, effectively making him the leader in their partnership?

Some people's main church role is to mentor someone with gifts far beyond their own, but such a responsibility is worthwhile before God. Pray for those called to such work.

MARTIN LECKEBUSCH

Saturday 30 August Acts 15:1–2, 6, 12 (TNIV, abridged)

Hard questions

Certain individuals came down from Judea to Antioch and were teaching the believers: 'Unless you are circumcised, according to the custom taught by Moses, you cannot be saved.' This brought Paul and Barnabas into sharp dispute and debate with them. So Paul and Barnabas were appointed… to go up to Jerusalem to see the apostles and elders about this question… The apostles and elders met to consider this question… The whole assembly became silent as they listened to Barnabas and Paul telling about the signs and wonders God had done among the Gentiles through them.

How could people with no Jewish heritage be welcomed into the church whose first members, like Jesus, were all Jewish? Must Gentile converts follow the law of Moses, which had shaped the life of God's people for centuries? Such questions were important, complex and potentially divisive in those days. The hard line being advocated by some traditionally minded visitors from Judea caused bewilderment in Antioch. Paul and Barnabas argued vigorously from a different perspective.

This chapter summarises a significant meeting in Jerusalem, called to discuss the issue. Barnabas and Paul were among the key participants. Their account of fruitful preaching to Gentile hearers provided an eye-opening moment for many of those present. What these two had done probably looked radical, but their audience had to admit that God had used them even though they had not pressed the Mosaic law's demands.

A consensus was reached, and the church moved forward. Those particular questions no longer cause controversy, but difficult ethical and theological questions still arise. It is therefore worth noting how those believers met together, listened to one another, explained their different experiences of God's grace and looked at what the scriptures said, to help them reach a common mind. The care they showed in their deliberations still offers us a valuable example.

Father, give your people wisdom for handling difficult questions and painful disagreements; help us to listen carefully, to learn from your Spirit and one another, and to discern your way forward together. Amen.

MARTIN LECKEBUSCH

Sunday 31 August — Acts 15:36–41 (TNIV, abridged)

A painful parting

Some time later Paul said to Barnabas, 'Let us go back and visit the believers in all the towns where we preached... and see how they are doing.' Barnabas wanted to take John, also called Mark, with them, but Paul did not think it wise to take him, because he had deserted them in Pamphylia... They had such a sharp disagreement that they parted company. Barnabas took Mark and sailed for Cyprus, but Paul chose Silas and left, commended by the believers to the grace of the Lord. He went through Syria and Cilicia, strengthening the churches.

Sadly, Barnabas and Paul's productive collaboration foundered, not over doctrinal differences, but over personalities. Barnabas, always the encourager, wanted to extend a second chance to John Mark, even though he had let them down on their first mission journey, abandoning them early on. Paul adamantly rejected the idea. The fact that Barnabas and Mark were related probably complicated matters still further. Unable to see how they could work together, Barnabas and Paul separated.

We cannot tell how widely their disagreement affected the church, either in Antioch or elsewhere. Luke notes that Paul and Silas' new endeavour was endorsed by the church, but does not say that about Barnabas' plans. Conversely, this painful parting did mean there were now two itinerant teams spreading the gospel, instead of one.

This is, however, not the end of the story. Some years afterwards, Paul may be alluding to these events at the end of Colossians. If so, he implies there that bygones should be bygones: Mark should be welcomed if he visits Colossae (Colossians 4:10). Later still, probably during his final earthly months, Paul asks Timothy to bring Mark to him, speaking positively of his assistance (2 Timothy 4:11). It seems Paul recognises that Barnabas' faith in Mark and willingness to mentor him have proved fruitful, making Mark a reliable co-worker.

Lord, thank you for those who have patiently encouraged my spiritual growth. Help me, likewise, to see and to foster my brothers' and sisters' potential. Amen.

MARTIN LECKEBUSCH

SHARING OUR VISION – MAKING A GIFT

I would like to make a donation to support BRF Ministries.
Please use my gift for:

☐ Where the need is greatest ☐ Anna Chaplaincy ☐ Living Faith
☐ Messy Church ☐ Parenting for Faith

Title	First name/initials	Surname

Address

Postcode

Email

Telephone

Signature | Date

Please accept my gift of:

☐ £2 ☐ £5 ☐ £10 ☐ £20 Other £ _____

by (*delete as appropriate*):

☐ Cheque/Charity Voucher payable to 'BRF'
☐ MasterCard/Visa/Debit card/Charity card

Name on card

Card no. ☐☐☐☐ ☐☐☐☐ ☐☐☐☐ ☐☐☐☐

Expires end MM YY Security code* ☐☐☐ *Last 3 digits on the reverse of the card

Signature | Date

Please complete other side of form ➡

SHARING OUR VISION – MAKING A GIFT

BRF Ministries Gift Aid Declaration

In order to Gift Aid your donation, you must tick the box below.

☐ I want to Gift Aid my donation and any donation I make in the future or have made in the past four years to BRF Ministries

I am a UK taxpayer and understand that if I pay less Income Tax and/or Capital Gains Tax in the current tax year than the amount of Gift Aid claimed on all my donations, it is my responsibility to pay any difference.

Please notify BRF Ministries if you want to cancel this Gift Aid declaration, change your name or home address, or no longer pay sufficient tax on your income and/or capital gains.

You can also give online at **brf.org.uk/donate**, which reduces our administration costs, making your donation go further.

Our ministry is only possible because of the generous support of individuals, churches, trusts and gifts in wills.

☐ I would like to leave a gift to BRF Ministries in my will.
   Please send me further information.

☐ I would like to find out about giving a regular gift to BRF Ministries.

For help or advice regarding making a gift, please contact our fundraising team +44 (0)1235 462305

Your privacy

We will use your personal data to process this transaction. From time to time we may send you information about the work of BRF Ministries that we think may be of interest to you. Our privacy policy is available at **brf.org.uk/privacy**. Please contact us if you wish to discuss your mailing preferences.

Registered with
FR
FUNDRAISING **REGULATOR**

↶ Please complete other side of form

Please return this form to 'Freepost BRF'
No other address information or stamp is needed

Bible Reading Fellowship is a charity (233280) and company limited by guarantee (301324), registered in England and Wales

Overleaf... Reading *New Daylight* in a group | Author profile | Recommended reading | Order and subscription forms

Reading *New Daylight* in a group

GORDON GILES

It is good to talk. While the Rule of Benedict, which formed the spiritual foundations of so many ecclesiastical foundations, recommended daily scripture reading as a key aspect of the community life of work and prayer, during Lent especially each monk was allocated a book to read daily. Benedict's monks did not talk much, but nowadays discussion and reflection can be helpful and enlightening when reading passages that others are simultaneously also reading. Separated by space, as each reads alone, we are yet connected by the common food of scripture, taken in our own time at our own pace. We each chew on it in our own way, and we can all learn from each other's insights and interpretations. To assist with that, here are some open questions that may enable discussion in a Bible study or other group who gather to take further what is published here. The same questions may also aid personal devotion too. Use them as you wish, and may God bless you on your journey as you read, mark and inwardly digest holy words to ponder and nourish the soul.

General discussion starters

These can be used for any study series within this issue. There are no right or wrong answers – these questions are simply to enable conversation.

- What do you think is the main idea or theme of the author in this series? Did that come across strongly?
- Have any of the issues discussed touched on personal – or shared – aspects of your life?
- What evidence or stories do the authors draw on to illuminate, or be illuminated by, the passages of scripture?
- Which do you prefer: scripture informing daily modern life or modern life shining a new light on scripture?
- Does the author call you to action in a realistic and achievable way? Do you think their ideas will work in the secular world?
- Have any specific passages struck you personally? If so, how and why? Is God speaking to you through scripture and reflection?
- Was anything completely new to you? Any 'eureka' or jaw-dropping moments? If so, what difference will that make?

Questions for discussion

1—3 John (Michael Mitton)

- Which of the ten words have taken on a new significance for you through these readings, and why?
- John speaks of having been physically present with Jesus. If John could be with you now, what questions would you ask about Jesus? How do you think John would have replied?
- John starts his first letter telling us about this wonderful gift of life in Christ. How is this life different from everyday life?
- John writes in no uncertain terms about the problems of sin and evil in this world. How can we live as those who recognise the problems of the world, yet not be overwhelmed or depressed by them?
- John uses the expression 'walking' referring to light, truth and love. How can we help each other keep to these three important pathways?
- Why do we find it so difficult to show the kind of *agapē* love that John frequently commends in his letters? How can such a quality of love take root in us and in our churches?

Esther (Fiona Stratta)

- In your life how have you seen the interplay between God's sovereignty and your choices and actions?
- Mordecai was at the right place at the right time and Esther responded to a calling for 'such a time as this'. These God-incidences of timing and apparent coincidence can be described as non-miraculous miracles. When have you experienced these in your life?
- Esther was sustained by God and the support of Mordecai and Hegai. When did God sustain you in dark times? What did you learn and who gave you support?
- One of the themes of Esther is the need to take a stand against injustice. What could 'acting justly, loving mercy and walking humbly with God' (Micah 6:8) look like in your life?
- The outcomes of God's deliverance are so much more than Esther and Mordecai could have imagined, giving them power to work for

good on behalf of the empire. How has God answered your prayers in ways you could not have imagined? How has this opened areas of influence for you to bless others?
- How does remembering and celebrating help you in your Christian journey?

Psalms 67—72 (Roland Riem)

- How do we guard against 'us' from becoming 'them and us'?
- What in worship together helps to remind us that God cares for his people?
- When is it right to be triumphant?
- How do we move from wishing retribution to wishing reconciliation?
- How is your desire for godly governance expressed in your own church's prayer and ministry?

Luke 13—16 (Margaret Silf)

- Are we losing the ability to wait in our 'instant' society? How might we regain the gift of patience? How might the scriptures, the sacred seasons and the rhythms of the natural world help us?
- Is there anything in your own life that God may be inviting you to let go of because it is hindering your spiritual journey? What do you feel our society in general needs to let go of if it is to grow in holiness?
- In the parable of the prodigal son do you find yourself sympathising with one of the brothers more than the other? What do you learn from your response? How do you feel about the father's reaction? Does the father in the story reflect something of your understanding of God?
- What does 'carrying the cross' mean to you?
- Where do you find yourself in the continual struggle between the attraction of material possessions or comfort and the attraction of God. Have there been times in your experience when you have had to choose?

Meet the author: Fiona Stratta

How did you come to faith and what were the earliest influences on your Christian journey?

I was brought up in a Christian family, attending church and Sunday School and my faith grew as I did. Having said that, there were key moments in my childhood and teenage years that stand out. I remember crying as a young child while singing in my bedroom 'There is a Green Hill Far Away', and singing from my heart 'Oh Jesus I Have Promised' at a Brownies event in Canterbury Cathedral. Of significance, too, were the Crusader (now Urban Saints) holidays that I attended as a teenager, including wonderful Easter morning services at a church on the Norfolk Broads. I made the commitment to go on with my family-led faith as my personal faith while attending Greenbelt Music and Arts Festival shortly before starting at university, and I was baptised not long afterwards.

My earliest influences would be from all those who told me Bible stories. This affinity to narrative has always been strong in me, and I can clearly remember 'standing in the corner' at Sunday School for a misdemeanour, which I imagine was 'over-contributing' to the story! My youth group and Crusader leaders were strong influences in my teenage years, encouraging and teaching me, as well as enabling me to develop Bible study and leadership skills. A further huge influence in my teenage years was the involvement of my family in a church plant. It was a sure way to see faith in action, observe answers to prayer and experience close fellowship.

Tell us about where you live, your church context and ministry.

I live in a beautiful west-country seaside town, where my husband and I attend the local Baptist church and where we brought up our two children (now with children of their own). I am comfortable in many church contexts. We used to live in the south-east and worshipped in a large county-town Anglican church. In my youth, my family worshipped in evangelical free churches. While at the University of Manchester, I loved the student Christian Union, went to an inner-city, multi-ethnic church, yet went for prayer and solitude into the beautiful, historic Catholic church situated among the university buildings. I have been blessed to experience these different traditions and have been greatly helped by Richard Foster's book *Streams of Living*

Water, which outlines six 'streams' of the Christian church – the contemplative, holiness, evangelical, social justice, charismatic and incarnational.

Over the years my church ministry has been with children and young people and as part of the worship group. Currently my husband and I co-lead one of the church's house groups. Actually, from Celtic Christianity I have come to see far less of a divide between the sacred and secular and view 'ministry' in a much broader sense. Much of it happens in the everyday: my earlier work as a speech and language therapist, my current work as a tutor and speech and drama teacher, and caring for the different generations in my family.

What have been the greatest joys and sorrows of your life and ministry?

Beyond my faith, great joys in my life are time with family and friends, singing, listening to and making music, a good book, creativity, writing, swimming, caravanning, and walking in the countryside and by the sea. Within ministry the greatest joys have been the involvement in the faith journeys of children and young people, and seeing the difference drama and language (spoken and written) can make in the lives of others. The sorrows have been family bereavements and heartaches, and a long period of poor health with associated losses of work, ministry and activities, although I am immensely blessed to live a carefully paced yet rich life, and I am grateful for the new opportunities that have opened up, such as writing.

What is your favourite book of the Bible and why?

John's gospel because of the way it tells of the life, words, death and resurrection of Jesus. I love the opening chapter, its truths and beauty, and also the richness and depth of the 'I am' sayings.

Which Bible character would you like to meet?

Primarily Jesus! There are so many others, but perhaps Martha. I would want to ask her how it went – this transformation from 'doing' to 'being'! It's a journey many of us find ourselves on.

If you could advise a younger generation, what would you say to them?

Stay in the moment – don't look back or forwards too much (except to learn from the past and appropriately plan for the future). To those who have a trust in and commitment to the Lord, I would give the advice I was given when leaving university: 'The most important thing is that the most important thing remains the most important thing.'

Recommended reading

Is this all there is to faith?

Every Christian carries a map, a mental image of their journey through life, created from their Christian tradition, their cultural background and their understanding of the Bible. Many Christians will also, at some point in their life, begin to question their map – causing them to ask, 'Is this all there is?' and 'How did I get here?'

Reimagining the Landscape of Faith
Essential pathways for spiritual growth

Mary and Charles Hippsley help us to identify our faith map, including the unexamined assumptions that underpin it. Then, drawing on a range of sources of wisdom, including personal experience, they gently encourage us to allow God to expand our map when we find that our faith doesn't match up with the reality of life. They aim to equip the reader to navigate their journey towards maturity by exploring new paths and landscapes of faith.

The following is an edited extract taken from the Introduction.

How do you feel about your journey of faith? Do you feel confident, sure-footed, that you know where you're going? Or perhaps you're a little uncertain, disappointed at where the path has taken you, or even lost. Maybe it would have been handy to have had a 'faith map', so that you could have planned your course and recognised some key landmarks as you travelled.

We all carry a kind of mental map of our spiritual journey, even if you are not aware that you do. As you delve deeper into this book, our hope is that you will learn not just how to recognise that map, but also how to critically evaluate it and begin to make choices based on a much deeper understanding of yourself and the nature of your map as you continue to journey with God.

But even when we are aware of having a map to hand, some of us still aren't sure how to read one or even which way up it should be! In my (Charles) many years of walking in the beautiful Lake District, the hardest part always seemed to be choosing the right direction to head out of the car park.

How are you reading your map, and what kind of faith landscape does it show?

Your map probably depicts familiar landmarks by which you navigate and measure progress on your faith pilgrimage. Symbolising the fundamentals of faith – such as orthodox beliefs and doctrines; regular personal and communal times of worship, prayer and sacraments; acts of evangelism, mission or social action – we consider our landmarks or milestones as being there to keep us on the 'right path', ever pointing towards God.

But here's a question to consider: are these common landmarks the only ones? They may seem fundamental, creating familiar rhythms of Christian life, but is there a possibility that your map is not yet complete? If you turned to the next page of your map, might you notice landmarks you haven't seen before, or could you even reimagine some old landmarks from time to time, sparked by changes in your experience or understanding? Might there be there some benefit in looking beyond your familiar routes to identify some even deeper and more significant pathways?

So, how might this book help you?

This book arises out of our experience as trained spiritual directors. While this is a well-established historical ministry, the art of spiritual direction may be less familiar within some Christian traditions. It's a different way of listening that helps people to notice what may lie beneath the surface of what's going on in their lives, to discern and interpret how God might be working towards their spiritual growth. We encourage people to ask themselves good questions, to take intentional notice of the landscape through which they are travelling and to pay attention to the feelings which arise.

A key part of this process is to encourage the active use of their God-given imagination as they explore the roots of their beliefs and expectations, facilitating both better self-awareness and God-awareness.

We find this approach to be helpful because having had many conversations with people who are wrestling with their faith, we noticed that they tend to be strongly influenced by both recognised and unrecognised expectations for their spiritual journey. These expectations often colour our perceptions of what's happening along the way.

Philip Yancey helpfully summarises some common hopes for the life of faith saying:

I want God to… overcome my doubts with certainty, give final proofs of his existence and his concern. I want quick and spectacular answers to prayers, healing for my diseases, protection, and safety for my loved ones.

So it won't be a surprise to learn that we will be inviting you as a reader to become more conscious of your secret hopes and often hidden inner world, activate your imagination, identify your feelings and participate in asking yourself some good questions. But rather than leave all those questions until the end of each chapter, we will weave them into key ideas, inviting you to reflect on how what we're sharing applies to your own faith journey as we go.

We're also exploring how a variety of disciplines must work in coordination if we are to fully grasp the contours of our maps of faith, especially if we want to grow spiritually. These include theology, spirituality, psychology and epistemology (how truth is pursued and perceived). When these aspects of our faith come together, it can be hugely enriching. Realising that we are not experts in all these disciplines, we have drawn on a range of those who are, many of whom you can find referenced in the endnotes and suggested reading list at the back of the book. But our overall aim is to highlight and integrate an awareness of where our Christian beliefs have come from together with an understanding of the humanity (heart, mind, body and spirit) with which we engage those beliefs.

To order a copy of this book, please use the order form or visit **brfonline.org.uk**

Enjoy a little luxury: upgrade to *New Daylight deluxe*

Many readers enjoy the compact format of the regular *New Daylight* but more and more people are discovering the advantages of the larger format, premium edition, *New Daylight deluxe.* The pocket-sized version is perfect if you're reading on the move but the larger print, white paper and extra space to write your own notes and comments all make the deluxe edition an attractive alternative and significant upgrade.

Why not try it to see if you like it? You can order single copies at brfonline.org.uk/newdaylightdeluxe

Deluxe actual size:

gladness instead of mourning, the mantle of spirit. They will be called oaks of righteousness, to display his glory.

We learn from these verses that gladness is first them' gladness instead of mourning and praise in gift needs to be received, and action is often re gift. For example, receiving a piano is of little u play it. God has blessed us with 'every spiritual but, metaphorically speaking, *we* have to pour o put on and wear the mantle of praise. The Lord

To order

Online: **brfonline.org.uk**
Telephone: +44 (0)1865 319700
Mon–Fri 9.30–17.00

Delivery times within the UK are normally 15 working days. Prices are correct at the time of going to press but may change without prior notice.

BRF

Title	Price	Qty	Total
Rhythms of Grace	£9.99		
The Poetry of Pilgrimage	£12.99		
Restoring the Woven Cord	£9.99		
Reimagining the Landscape of Faith	£12.99		
The Works of the Lord	£12.99		

POSTAGE AND PACKING CHARGES			
Order value	UK	Europe	Rest of world
Under £7.00	£2.00	Available on request	Available on request
£7.00–£29.99	£3.00		
£30.00 and over	FREE		

Total value of books	
Postage and packing	
Donation*	
Total for this order	

* Please complete and return the Gift Aid declaration on page 142.

Please complete in BLOCK CAPITALS

Title .... First name/initials .... Surname ....

Address ....

.... Postcode ....

Acc. No. .... Telephone ....

Email ....

Method of payment

❏ Cheque (made payable to BRF) ❏ MasterCard / Visa

Card no. ☐☐☐☐ ☐☐☐☐ ☐☐☐☐ ☐☐☐☐

Expires end M M Y Y   Security code ☐☐☐   Last 3 digits on the reverse of the card

We will use your personal data to process this order. From time to time we may send you information about the work of BRF Ministries. Please contact us if you wish to discuss your mailing preferences. Our privacy policy is available at **brf.org.uk/privacy**.

Please return this form to:
BRF Ministries, 15 The Chambers, Vineyard, Abingdon OX14 3FE | **enquiries@brf.org.uk**
For terms and cancellation information, please visit **brfonline.org.uk/terms**.

Bible Reading Fellowship (BRF) is a charity (233280) and company limited by guarantee (301324), registered in England and Wales

BRF Ministries needs you!

If you're one of our many thousands of regular *New Daylight* readers you will know all about the benefits and blessings of regular Bible reading and the value of daily notes to guide, inform and inspire you. Here are some recent comments from *New Daylight* readers:

> *'Thank you for all the many inspiring writings that help so much when things are tough.'*
>
> *'Just right for me – I learned a lot!'*
>
> *'We looked forward to each day's message as we pondered each passage and comment.'*

If you have similarly positive things to say about *New Daylight*, would you be willing to share your experience with others? Could you ask for a brief slot during church notices or write a short piece for your church magazine or website? Do you belong to groups, formal or informal, where you could share your experience of using Bible reading notes and encourage others to try them?

It doesn't need to be complicated or nerve-wracking: just answering these three questions in what you say or write will get your message across:

- How do Bible reading notes help you grow in your faith?
- Where, when and how do you use them?
- What would you say to people who don't already use them?

We can supply further information if you need it and would love to hear about it if you do give a talk or write an article.

For more information:

- Email **enquiries@brf.org.uk**
- Phone us on **+44 (0)1865 319700** Mon–Fri 9.30–17.00
- Write to us at BRF Ministries, 15 The Chambers, Vineyard, Abingdon OX14 3FE

Inspiring people of all ages to grow in Christian faith

At BRF Ministries, we long for people of all ages to grow in faith and understanding of the Bible. That's what all our work as a charity is about.

- Our **Living Faith** range of resources helps Christians go deeper in their understanding of scripture, in prayer and in their walk with God. Our conferences and events bring people together to share this journey, while our Holy Habits resources help whole congregations grow together as disciples of Jesus, living out and sharing their faith.
- We also want to make it easier for local churches to engage effectively in ministry and mission – by helping them bring new families into a growing relationship with God through **Messy Church** or by supporting churches as they nurture the spiritual life of older people through **Anna Chaplaincy**.
- Our **Parenting for Faith** team coaches parents and others to raise God-connected children and teens, and enables churches to fully support them.

Do you share our vision?

Though a significant proportion of BRF Ministries' funding is generated through our charitable activities, we are dependent on the generous support of individuals, churches and charitable trusts.

If you share our vision, would you help us to enable even more people of all ages to grow in faith? Your prayers and financial support are vital for the work that we do. You could:

- support us with a regular donation or one-off gift
- consider leaving a gift to BRF Ministries in your will
- encourage your church to support us as part of your church's giving to home mission – perhaps focusing on a specific ministry or programme
- most important of all, support us with your prayers.

Donate at **brf.org.uk/donate** or use the form on pages 141–42.

United in Christ

'Divided tongues, as of fire, appeared among them, and a tongue rested on each of them. All of them were filled with the Holy Spirit and began to speak in other languages, as the Spirit gave them ability.'
ACTS 2:3–4 (NRSV)

This edition covers the period of Ascensiontide and Pentecost, a time for marvelling at the wonder of Christ's ascension to heaven and the Spirit being sent down to be with us all, uniting us in Christ, beyond the boundaries of countries and languages.

Our Messy Church team are deep in the reality of this worldwide community of faith, with the Messy Church International Conference 2025 and Key Leaders Gathering. These events take a huge amount of planning, and we are grateful to all who have been involved in making them happen.

The Anna Chaplaincy, Living Faith and Parenting for Faith teams are equally busy with running training courses, attending conferences, bringing people together, and equipping and resourcing people in their ministries and everyday lives.

None of this would be possible without the faith-filled generosity of our supporters. Regular giving, one-off donations, gifts in wills, grants from charitable trusts, responses to appeals, and top-up donations with purchases or event bookings – every single gift helps us provide the resources that touch lives around the world. Thank you.

Find out more at **brf.org.uk/donate** or get in touch with us on **01235 462305** or via **giving@brf.org.uk**

The fundraising team at BRF Ministries

> Give. Pray. Get involved.
> **brf.org.uk**

NEW DAYLIGHT SUBSCRIPTION RATES

Please note our new subscription rates, current until 30 April 2026:

Individual subscriptions
covering 3 issues for under 5 copies, payable in advance
(including postage & packing):

	UK	Europe	Rest of world
New Daylight	£21.30	£29.55	£35.25
New Daylight Deluxe per set of 3 issues p.a.	£26.55	£36.00	£44.10

Group subscriptions
covering 3 issues for 5 copies or more, sent to one UK address (post free):

New Daylight	£15.75 per set of 3 issues p.a.
New Daylight Deluxe	£19.50 per set of 3 issues p.a.

Please note that the annual billing period for group subscriptions runs from 1 May to 30 April.

Overseas group subscription rates
Available on request. Please email **enquiries@brf.org.uk**.

Copies may also be obtained from Christian bookshops:

New Daylight	£5.25 per copy
New Daylight Deluxe	£6.50 per copy

> All our Bible reading notes can be ordered online by visiting **brfonline.org.uk/subscriptions**

NEW DAYLIGHT INDIVIDUAL SUBSCRIPTION FORM

To set up a recurring subscription, please go to
brfonline.org.uk/new-daylight

Title .... First name/initials .... Surname ....

Address ....

.... Postcode ....

Telephone .... Email ....

Please send *New Daylight* beginning with the September 2025 / January 2026 / May 2026 issue (*delete as appropriate*):

(*please tick box*)	UK	Europe	Rest of world
New Daylight	☐ £21.30	☐ £29.55	☐ £35.25
New Daylight Deluxe	☐ £26.55	☐ £36.00	☐ £44.10

Optional donation to support the work of BRF Ministries £ ....

Total enclosed £ .... (cheques should be made payable to 'BRF')

Please complete and return the Gift Aid declaration on page 142 to make your donation even more valuable to us.

Please charge my MasterCard / Visa with £ ....

Card no. ☐☐☐☐ ☐☐☐☐ ☐☐☐☐ ☐☐☐☐

Expires end M M Y Y   Security code ☐☐☐   Last 3 digits on the reverse of the card

We will use your personal data to process this order. From time to time we may send you information about the work of BRF Ministries. Please contact us if you wish to discuss your mailing preferences. Our privacy policy is available at **brf.org.uk/privacy**.

Please return this form with the appropriate payment to:
BRF Ministries, 15 The Chambers, Vineyard, Abingdon OX14 3FE
For terms and cancellation information, please visit **brfonline.org.uk/terms**.

Bible Reading Fellowship is a charity (233280) and company limited by guarantee (301324), registered in England and Wales

NEW DAYLIGHT GIFT SUBSCRIPTION FORM

☐ I would like to give a gift subscription (please provide both names and addresses):

Title .... First name/initials .... Surname ....

Address ....

.... Postcode ....

Telephone .... Email ....

Gift subscription name ....

Gift subscription address ....

.... Postcode ....

Gift message (20 words max. or include your own gift card):

....

....

Please send *New Daylight* beginning with the September 2025 / January 2026 / May 2026 issue (*delete as appropriate*):

(please tick box)	UK	Europe	Rest of world
New Daylight	☐ £21.30	☐ £29.55	☐ £35.25
New Daylight Deluxe	☐ £26.55	☐ £36.00	☐ £44.10

Optional donation to support the work of BRF Ministries £ ....

Total enclosed £ .... (cheques should be made payable to 'BRF')

Please complete and return the Gift Aid declaration on page 142 to make your donation even more valuable to us.

Please charge my MasterCard / Visa with £ ....

Card no. ☐☐☐☐ ☐☐☐☐ ☐☐☐☐ ☐☐☐☐

Expires end ☐☐ ☐☐   Security code ☐☐☐   Last 3 digits on the reverse of the card

We will use your personal data to process this order. From time to time we may send you information about the work of BRF Ministries. Please contact us if you wish to discuss your mailing preferences. Our privacy policy is available at **brf.org.uk/privacy**.

Please return this form with the appropriate payment to:
BRF Ministries, 15 The Chambers, Vineyard, Abingdon OX14 3FE
For terms and cancellation information, please visit **brfonline.org.uk/terms**.

Bible Reading Fellowship is a charity (233280) and company limited by guarantee (301324), registered in England and Wales

BRF Ministries

Inspiring people of all ages to grow in Christian faith

BRF Ministries is the home of Anna Chaplaincy, Living Faith, Messy Church and Parenting for Faith

As a charity, our work would not be possible without fundraising and gifts in wills.
To find out more and to donate, visit brf.org.uk/give or call +44 (0)1235 462305

Registered with FUNDRAISING REGULATOR